THE STORIES JESUS TOLD

Lessons from the Parables of Jesus

LIFE TO LEGACY, LLC

Life2Legacy.com

The Stories Jesus Told:
Lessons from the Parables of Jesus
Copyright © 2015 Larry A. Brookins
for LA Brookins Ministries

ISBN-13 978-1-939654-58-8

Editor: Charlotte Brookins-Hudson, Esq.

Cover Image: BLACK ART IN AMERICA, LLC:
1506 Sixth Avenue #119,
Columbus, Georgia 31901,
www.blackartinamerica.com

Printed in the United States
10 9 8 7 6 5 4 3 2 1

Library of Congress Control Number: 2015940132

Published by: Life To Legacy, LLC
877-267-7477
Life2legacybooks@att.net

TESTIMONIALS

"I have had the privilege of utilizing Rev. Dr. Larry A. Brookins' manuscripts, books, and workbooks as an aide in my own sermon preparation. I find them very insightful and powerful tools and study instruments. Dr. Brookins writings are both straightforward and engaging, and when used properly, can help save study and research time thereby simplifying your sermon preparation. His discerning awareness and scripture application assists me in painting a picture in vivid and easily understandable terms."

—Pastor Leon Washington ~ Woodbine, Georgia

All I can say is that Rev. Dr. Larry A. Brookins' publications, "Becoming a Five-Star Member" and "Becoming a Five-Star Church" was a tremendous blessing. I highly recommend both of them.

—Pastor Corinthian R. Morgan ~ Jacksonville, Florida

Rev. Dr. Larry A. Brookins is truly one of God's most gifted, insightful, inspirational, prolific, dynamic, and anointed God inspired and Spirit filled writers of our time. I highly recommend all of his written material, including his books, "It's All about the Kingdom, Volume One," "Seven Things that God Hates," and "The Detox Series." These are a must read for every pastor, preacher, and even layperson.

—Dr. Homer Jamison ~ Detroit, Michigan

Dr. Brookins' messages are inspiring and powerful. I am delighted to have the opportunity to read, and many times, borrow some of the profound statements from his work(s). One cannot come across such in-depth and challenging words as his. I must say that his language and research is golden and precious. To him I say "thanks."

—Rev. Marvel M. Williams ~ Little Rock, Arkansas

THANKS & DEDICATION

Let me first thank my sister, my editor, Charlotte Brookins-Hudson, for her untiring devotion to editing this book. She deleted, inserted, amended, and gave herself unselfishly to this project. She improved my phrases and punctuations and kept me from plagiarism infringements. I guess its advantageous having a sister who is a lawyer. Charlotte, you make me better. Words cannot express how I appreciate your labors of love and assistance. The only word I can think of to say is THANKS!

To my parents, wife, children, siblings, grandchildren, friends, TFTC church members, and every benefactor of LA Brookins Ministries (L.A.B.M.), I value every word of encouragement and seed of support. I must, however, give honorable mention to my fabulous L.A.B.M. team: Renee K. Robinson, and Sammie and Debra Robinson, who travel with me, sacrifice for me, and work so hard in helping me in the set up and sale of our books, workbooks, manuals, manuscripts, and sermon CDs and DVDs. I also thank Dorothy Scales, Margaret Battee, and Vivian Whiteside, who assist us in preparing all materials for transport. You guys are fantastic! I cannot do what I do without any of you.

Finally, I dedicate this book to the memory of my brother-in-law, Huey L. Johnson, who meant so much to so many. He gave himself to family, friends, his church, his God, and to the cause of Christ. I so miss him, but I know I shall see him again. He would have been so proud and happy, and among the first in line to get this book. I love you Huey! Never forgotten! Always with us!

TABLE OF CONTENTS

Foreword

Seventeenth Century mathematician and physicist Sir Isaac Newton once said, "If I have seen further than others, it is by standing upon the shoulders of giants." In any field of study—whether it be philosophy, science, or theology—we have the benefit of building upon the body of work and research of those who have labored before us. It is upon this basis that Dr. Newton's quote is very well applicable to Dr. Larry A. Brookins, a consummate exegete, expositor, professor, pastor, and preacher. Dr. Brookins' voluminous body of expository work has enabled countless ministers, pastors, and teachers to see further.

When prolific authors are asked what is their favorite among their literary works, they often respond by saying that it is their latest work. The Stories Jesus Told: Lessons from the Parables of Jesus, Dr. Brookins' latest rendering, is a treasure trove of knowledge filled with golden nuggets of wisdom and truth that now finds itself in a prominent position among his other theological works. Dr. Brookins is very much a preacher's preacher and a teacher's teacher, and his writings have been the homiletic and hermeneutic source material for sermons preached and Bible studies taught throughout the United States.

In view of the fact that Dr. Brookins' literary style is both didactic and digestible, his writings are much in demand by laypersons and church leaders alike. This book is a relevant and timely work that gives the substance of Jesus' parabolic teachings without inundating the reader with endless theological abstractions. What Dr. Brookins has accomplished in this engaging work is to give the reader a commentary that is equally as enjoyable as it is informative. In my opinion, that is the mark of biblical exposition at its best.

—Dr. Dennis J. Woods
President/CEO
Life To Legacy, LLC
and Pastor of Power of the Holy Ghost
Deliverance Ministries,
Chicago, Illinois

INTRODUCTION

"Hey, did you hear the one about . . . !" People love a good story. Stories capture our imagination, stir our emotions, impact us in ways that precepts and propositions never do, as they arrest our attention, peak our interest, engage our mind, and excite our spirit and soul—from the youngest of us to the oldest of us. Stories have a way of helping us to learn, especially a story with pictures.

Jesus was a great storyteller! In fact, He was the best. His stories were not told to entertain His audience or to arouse the flesh, but to communicate spiritual truth with illustrations known to those around Him. The stories Jesus told were God-inspired and designed to bring revelation, inspiration, education, and even conviction. They were crafted to be easily remembered, as the characters were bold and narratives rich in symbolic meaning.

Storytelling was Jesus' favorite method of teaching, and oh when He taught, the crowd around Him listened, both those who endeared Him, as well as those who opposed Him. The testimony of John 7:46 is, *"No one ever spoke like this Man"*! Oftentimes, the motivation for His stories was the hypocrisy, arrogance, and resistance of the religious leaders (Pharisees, Sadducees, Scribes, Elders and Priests), but Jesus also told them to open up the mysteries of God's Kingdom to His faithful followers, while concealing these divine secrets from His antagonists (see Matthew 13:10-17).

At one point in His ministry Jesus did not teach without the inclusion of a story (see Matthew 13:34-35), and His stories were spoken with simple language that utilized familiar situations, events and things that were common: birds, flowers, loss, livestock, farming, debt, family, inheritance, wealth, investment, servanthood, service, marriage, relationship, charity, character, prayer, Heaven, Hell, and so much more. In His stories, Jesus did not use theological vocabulary, but terms that the average person, no matter the educational level, gender, social status, or age could comprehend. These stories were known as "parables."

Parables are metaphorical stories. A "metaphor" is "a word, phrase or thing that is regarded as representative of something else." It is a figure of speech that makes an implicit comparison of objects, ideas, thoughts, or feelings in order to provide a clearer description or complete interpretation of connotation. The earliest definition of a parable I was given is: "an earthly story with a Heavenly meaning." The parables of Jesus have one central point, which differ from storyline to storyline, but they are all intended to explain what the Kingdom of God is like and what is expected of those so privileged to be a part of the Kingdom family. In fact, some parables start off with the phrase, *"the Kingdom of Heaven is like...."* Note Matthew Chapter Thirteen.

I pray that the lessons God gave me, via these parables, will continue to uplift, inform, inspire, and encourage, as they did when I preached them. As best as possible I have tried to maintain the integrity of what I preached; however, because these lessons are now put into publication, I have taken the liberty to insert Biblical references where quoted for research, reword some phrases for better reading, as well as to give author credit to those statements I have borrowed from other sources. This book is a book for everyone. Preachers can preach them. Teachers can teach them. Christians can share them. Sinners can learn from them. These are the stories Jesus told, and there is a lesson in each one. FINAL NOTE: The parables contained within this collection are not all of Jesus' parables, but those selected by the dictate of the Holy Spirit. Enjoy. Be edified. Listen and learn from the Master Storyteller—Jesus. It is He who said, *"He who has ears to hear, let him hear"* (Matthew 11:15)!

—Rev. Dr. Larry A. Brookins

He taught them by telling many
stories in the form of parables

Mark 4:2, NLT

CHAPTER 1

THE 'RIGHT SIDE' IS THE RIGHT SIDE

The Parable of the Sheep and the Goats

Matthew 25:31-46

[31] When the Son of Man comes in His glory, and all the holy angels with Him, then He will sit on the throne of His glory. [32] All the nations will be gathered before Him, and He will separate them one from another, as a shepherd divides his sheep from the goats. [33] And He will set the sheep on His right hand, but the goats on the left. [34] Then the King will say to those on His right hand, 'Come, you blessed of My Father, inherit the kingdom prepared for you from the foundation of the world: [35] for I was hungry and you gave Me food; I was thirsty and you gave Me drink; I was a stranger and you took Me in; [36] I was naked and you clothed Me; I was sick and you visited Me; I was in prison and you came to Me.' [37] "Then the righteous will answer Him, saying, 'Lord, when did we see You hungry and feed You, or thirsty and give You drink? [38] When did we see You a stranger and take You in, or naked and clothe You? [39] Or when did we see You sick, or in prison, and come to You?' [40] And the King will answer and say to them, 'Assuredly, I say to you, inasmuch as you did it to one

of the least of these My brethren, you did it to Me.' [41] "Then He will also say to those on the left hand, 'Depart from Me, you cursed, into the everlasting fire prepared for the devil and his angels: [42] for I was hungry and you gave Me no food; I was thirsty and you gave Me no drink; [43] I was a stranger and you did not take Me in, naked and you did not clothe Me, sick and in prison and you did not visit Me.' [44] "Then they also will answer Him, saying, 'Lord, when did we see You hungry or thirsty or a stranger or naked or sick or in prison, and did not minister to You?' [45] Then He will answer them, saying, 'Assuredly, I say to you, inasmuch as you did not do it to one of the least of these, you did not do it to Me.' [46] And these will go away into everlasting punishment, but the righteous into eternal life.

Set before us is a parable of Jesus. A *parable* is a simple story that employs metaphors of things that are familiar to the hearer. A *metaphor* is simply a word, phrase or thing that is regarded as representative or symbolic of something else. It is a figure of speech that makes an implicit comparison of two unlike objects, ideas, thoughts or feelings in order to provide a clearer description or more complete interpretation of meaning. A *parable* is designed to communicate a spiritual truth or principle. In other words, it seeks to teach a lesson utilizing earthly matters to impart a divine lesson. In fact, most parables have one central point, especially the parables of Jesus.

Jesus was a master of the parabolic method of teaching. Jesus was an expert in story-telling. In fact, much of what He taught, especially during the latter stages of His ministry, was by way of *parable*. Mark 4:2 says, *"And He taught them many things by parables."* In this, per Don Schwager, "Jesus used simple word-pictures, called parables, to help people understand who God is and what His Kingdom or reign is like" (*The Parables of Jesus*). Jesus also used parables to communicate what is expected of all who would be a part of the Kingdom family.

In teaching by way of parables, Jesus employed imageries and personalities from everyday life to create a miniscule dramatization to illuminate His message. In teaching by way of parables, the stories of Jesus captivated an all-inclusive audience—young and old, rich and poor, and people who were educated, as well as illiterate. By telling stories about occupations, events, characters and objects everyone could understand, Jesus painted vivid portraits that apprehended the mind and imagination of His audience: *"A sower went out to sow." "A certain man had two sons." "The Kingdom of Heaven is like a net thrown into the sea." "Look at the fig tree." "Look at the birds in the air." "Look at the lilies of the field." "The Kingdom of Heaven is like a householder who went out early in the morning to hire laborers for his vineyard." "A certain creditor had two debtors."*

Jesus loved telling stories, and many of us understand that a good picture can speak more clearly than many words. Thus, Jesus used the ordinary to point to another order of reality that was hidden, yet visible to those who had *eyes to see and ears to hear*. In fact, much of the reason Jesus began to speak in parables was to discriminate between those who were open to receive what He taught and those who scoffed at Him and His teachings. This is irradiated in Matthew 13:10-17, Mark 4:10-12, and Luke 8:9-10. Jesus taught in parables to reveal truth to sincere seekers, while concealing the same truth from those who rejected Him. In fact, Jesus did what He instructs us to do. In Matthew 7:6 Jesus says, *"Don't waste what is holy on people who are unholy. Don't throw your pearls to pigs"* (NLT)! Scripture teaches us that a carnal or unreceptive mind cannot discern or recognize spiritual things (see 1 Corinthians 2:14).

The parables of Jesus are like buried treasure waiting to be discovered (see Matthew 13:44); their truth are only discovered by those who seek understanding. Those who seek understanding pray. Those who seek understanding study the Word of God. Those who seek understanding go to Sunday School. Those who seek understanding attend Bible Study. These are they who want to know what God requires of us. These are they who want to know more about God, His Son Jesus, and what being a Christian is all about. The Bible says, *"Blessed are those who hunger and thirst after righteousness, for they shall be filled"* (Matthew 5:6). My questions to you are: How hungry are you? How thirsty are you?

Over a third of the Gospels contain parables told by Jesus, and our text is one of these parables of Jesus. The focus is on meeting human needs. The focus is on demonstrating one's faith through rendering good deeds. In fact, this is the central point of the parable. The central point deals with how we treat each other, especially how we interact with individuals who lack the essentials of life, and with those who are in need of encouragement and or a word of inspiration or motivation. It seeks to expound to us what will be judged of us, and what will be considered as evidence of our faith in Jesus and love of Jesus. Jesus Himself said, *"If you love Me, keep My commandments"* (John 14:15).

The parable of Matthew 25:31-46 is more commonly known as *The Parable of the Sheep and the Goats*. It is labeled as such because of the allegorical language used within it to distinguish two categories of people—the sheep and the goats. The sheep being those branded as *the blessed*. The goats branded as *the cursed*; the sheep being placed on the right side, the goats on the left side. The sheep referred to as "the righteous," the goats as "the wicked." These metaphors are used because of the nature of sheep and goats. SHEEP are emblematic of mildness, simplicity, innocence, patience and usefulness. The people chosen as sheep nations, gathered to the right side, will be those who are charitable and capable of unconscious and unaffected goodness. These do what they do not to be seen or applauded by others, but simply to minister to needs and to fill voids in the lives of others. People with a sheep nature are compassionate, loving, kindhearted, and considerate. GOATS, unlike sheep, are naturally argumentative, lascivious, excessively ill-scented and symbolic of what is riotous, profane and impure. Innately selfish, goats represent nations gathered to the left side, who are given to their own passions and lusts, and who fail to see or respond to the needs of others. Goat people are unsympathetic, heartless, insensitive, and uncaring. Their only care is for themselves.

Notice within the context of Matthew 25:31-46, the sheep and the goats had the same opportunities to minister and to assist, but both did not have the same responses, actions, or reactions, which causes a separation of placement and pronouncement. Thus, judgment will be fair, accurate, unbiased and correct because we have the same opportunities to serve and minister. Jesus spoke this parable during His final week of ministry. Sometime during His final week, prior to His crucifixion, Jesus taught in the Temple at Jerusalem and answered challenges by various religious leaders. This exchange of challenge is recorded within chapters 21 through 23. Later, Jesus left the Temple and taught His disciples privately at the Mount of Olives. He told them what to expect in the future, both at the fall of Jerusalem and at the time of His Second Coming. Chapter 24 deals with this. Then here in chapter 25, Jesus tells three parables to show His disciples, inclusive of us, that they, and we, need to be ready when He returns. Indeed, He is coming back!

The first of the three parables of Chapter 25 is known as *The Parable of the Ten Virgins.* Five were foolish and five were wise. Five were ready and five were not. We shall deal with this parable in the next chapter. The second of the three parables is called *The Parable of the Talents.* In summary, when a certain master went away to "a far country," he gave each of his servants a number of talents (money). Upon his return, he summoned the servants together to find out what they had done with what he had given. We shall deal with this parable in future chapters. The third parable of this chapter was the climax of all that Jesus had been teaching about the end times. It is our *Parable of the Sheep and the Goats*, presenting us with a dramatic picture of Judgment Day— whether we care to believe it or not, we shall all see Judgment Day. In other words, we shall all stand before Christ and give an account of our stewardship and service. This will take place when Christ returns to usher in His reign. At that time, all righteous and unrighteous nations will be assembled, and both *rewards* and *punishments* will be announced. Unlike His lowly entrance into this world as a baby in Bethlehem, at His Second Coming, Jesus will appear in all His brilliant majesty. At that time, Jesus will sit on His Throne and all the holy angels will be with Him, and *as a shepherd divides his sheep from the goats, Jesus* shall separate the nations before Him. On His right He will gather the sheep, and to His left will go the goats. I know Beyoncé said, "To the left, to the left" (*Irreplaceable*, Beyoncé Knowles), but the 'right side' is the right side. Let me say, "To the right, to the right." *Judgment Day* is coming.

Judgment Day will be final exam day. It is a final exam with a six-part review: Part 1, how were we with the hungry? Part 2, how were we with the thirsty? Part 3, how were we with the stranger? Part 4, how were we with the naked? Part 5, how were we with the sick? Part 6, how were we with those behind prison bars? Did we care? Did we share? Did we visit? Did we help?

Our treatment of them will be deliberated by Jesus, for Jesus takes personal our treatment of them—on Judgment Day its judgment day. It will be "all rise." The final court will be in session. On *Judgment Day*, it is up to us whether we shall be found on the right side or the left side, based upon what we do now. The choice or choices we make now concludes the outcome then. Why now? People are hungry now. Why now? People are thirsty now. Why now? People are strangers now. Why now? People are naked now. People are sick now. People are imprisoned now. Whether or not we choose to minister to them determines our placement for Judgment Day. Be careful. The Bible says, *"Be not forgetful to entertain strangers: for thereby some have entertained angels unawares"* (Hebrews 13:2). Be careful.

The 'right side' is the right side, but it is the side of those who choose to feed the hungry, and the side of those who choose to clothe the naked, and the side of those who choose to take in the stranger, and the side of those who give drink to the thirsty, comfort the sick, and of those who take time to visit the imprisoned. It is the side of those who seek to do the will of God. It is the side of those who walk in the footsteps of Jesus. It is the side of those who deny themselves for the sake of others. It is the side reserved for them who don't mind helping someone else. The right side is for them whose theme song is, "If I can help somebody as I pass along; if I can cheer somebody with a word or song; if I can show somebody that they are traveling wrong" (*If I Can Help Somebody*, Mahalia Jackson). The 'right side' is the right side, but it is earmarked *for* givers, and for people who share and care, and who do what they can to put a smile on somebody's face, lift somebody's burdens, enliven somebody's heart, and brighten somebody's day. Jesus takes personal what we do or fail to do for somebody else. Inasmuch as we do or not do to others, we do or not do to Him. Jesus identifies with human need. He lived among us, faced our temptations, felt our pains, and experienced firsthand what it is like to be hungry, what it is like to be thirsty, what it is like to be homeless, and what it is like to be ignored. The Bible says, *"He came unto His own and His own received Him not"* (John 1:11).

The 'right side' is the right side, but it is up to us. It is up to me. It is up to you. It is up to us to do what we can to feed the hungry. It is up to us to clothe the naked. It is up to us to shelter the homeless. It is up to us to care for the sick. It is up to us to quench the thirst of the thirsty. It is up to us to visit the incarcerated. It is up to us to be approved or disapproved, to be rewarded or reprimanded, to be favored or rejected, to be invited in or closed out. It is up to us! And if you want to hear the Lord say, *"Servant, well done,"* *then* the 'right side' is the right side. If you want to make it into Heaven, then the 'right side' is the right side. The *right side* is the side of the faithful. The *right side* is the side of the merciful. The *right side* is the side of the gracious. It is the side for people who love people, for people who help people, for people who give to people, and for people who are good Samaritans to the downtrodden, ostracized, exploited, and those who are in need. The 'right side' is set aside for the ones who reach out and reach down, and to them Jesus will say, *"Come, ye blessed of My Father, inherit the Kingdom prepared for you from the foundation of the world"* (Matthew 25:34). Heaven is a prepared Place for a prepared people. Are you ready? Are you willing? Are you on the *right side*? Right side: APPROVED. Left side: CONDEMNED. Right side: FAVORED. Left side: REJECT-ED. Right side: SAVED. Left side: LOST. Right side: HEAV-EN. Left side: HELL. The 'right side' is the right side! To the right, to the right—MOVE OVER TO THE RIGHT SIDE!

CHAPTER 2

WILL YOU BE READY?

Parable of the Wise and Foolish Virgins

Matthew 25:1-13

[1]Then the kingdom of heaven shall be likened to ten virgins who took their lamps and went out to meet the bridegroom. [2] Now five of them were wise, and five were foolish. [3] Those who were foolish took their lamps and took no oil with them, [4] but the wise took oil in their vessels with their lamps. [5] But while the bridegroom was delayed, they all slumbered and slept. [6] "And at midnight a cry was heard: 'Behold, the bridegroom is coming; go out to meet him!' [7] Then all those virgins arose and trimmed their lamps. [8] And the foolish said to the wise, 'Give us some of your oil, for our lamps are going out.' [9] But the wise answered, saying, 'No, lest there should not be enough for us and you; but go rather to those who sell, and buy for yourselves.' [10] And while they went to buy, the bridegroom came, and those who were ready went in with him to the wedding; and the door was shut. [11] "After-

ward the other virgins came also, saying, 'Lord, Lord, open to us!' [12] But he answered and said, 'Assuredly, I say to you, I do not know you.'[13] "Watch therefore, for you know neither the day nor the hour in which the Son of Man is coming.

※※※

We turn our attention to another parable of Jesus. In fact, as we center our attention on one parable, we will elaborate on two parables—two parables that are connected—two parables with a common theme. The parable of Matthew 25:1-13 is called *The Parable of the Ten Virgins*, also known as *The Parable of the Wise and Foolish Virgins*. It is, perhaps, one of the best known of Jesus' parables, and as stated in Chapter One, it is one of a series of parables told by Jesus near the end of His ministry during a day of public teaching in the temple at Jerusalem, and in private the evening of the same day with His closest disciples, utilizing the seclusion of the Mount of Olives. So significant was this day and what Jesus said that Matthew devotes the majority of Chapters 21 through 25 to this busy day of public and private teaching. The primary subject matter of what was discussed and of all these interconnected parables centered on the end time and the Second Coming of Christ. What triggered this comprehensive discourse was a question posed to Jesus by His disciples.

As Jesus and the disciples were leaving the temple area at the end of the day headed toward the Mount of Olives, one of the disciples commented on the impressive stones of the temple building (see Matthew 24:1 or Mark 13:1). But rather than be impressed, Jesus startles the disciples with His response (see Matthew 24:2 or Mark 13:2). In reply, Jesus tells them that a day would come when the temple would be destroyed with no stone remaining upright. Thus, once they arrived at the seclusion of the Mount of Olives, the stunned disciples approached Jesus privately and asked Him to elaborate on what He said, as the Temple remained in view from where they assembled on the Mount of Olives. The account of Mark 13 identifies these inquisitive disciples as: Peter, James, John and Andrew. These four wanted Jesus to explain what He meant when He stated that the Temple would be destroyed with no stone remaining upright.   More specifically they asked Him, *"When will the Temple be destroyed, and what will be the sign that the end of the age has arrived"* (Matthew 24:3)? And this question gives rise to what is recorded in the remainder of Matthew 24, as well as it serves as the springboard for the parables of Matthew 25.

Some Bible students maintain that Matthew 24 predicts the fall of Jerusalem, inclusive of the destruction of the temple, which occurred in 70 A.D. at the hands of the Roman army. Still others insist that it focuses exclusively on signs that will foretell the end of time and the Second Coming of Christ. Most scholars see both interpretations, the fall of Jerusalem and the Second Coming of Christ, believing that Jesus alternates between the two, linking the two events together, prophesy the end of the temple as a foretaste of the end of the world, with the evidence of the temple destruction giving guarantee to the end of the world and the Second Coming of Christ. But, regardless of how one approaches Matthew 24, it is obvious by verse 36 that Jesus gives principal consideration to the end times and to the Day He will return to earth. There are a lot of people who theorize when that Day will be, but Jesus says *"Of that day and [of that] hour no one knows, not even the angels of Heaven, but My Father only"* (Matthew 24:36). In fact, the parables of Matthew 25: the *Parable of the Talents*, the *Parable of the Sheep and the Goats*, and for certain, the *Parable of the Ten Virgins do* not focus on urging us to seek signs, but to be ready when the Day arrives. In these entire parables one theme is clear—of that Day we have no pre-notice. In other words, of that Day we are not given a specific due date to prepare for. In other words, the Second Coming of Christ will not be announced in advance so we can plan on when to get our lives ready for the Judgment. To the contrary, the parable of Matthew 25:1-13 encourages us to stay ready at all times, always recognizing that today, or tomorrow's today, could be the Day that Jesus returns. One thing is certain—one day some living generation in earth's history will experience that Day. Also one thing is certain—it will occur when least expected. Again, no one knows the day or the hour but God. In life two things are certain: Jesus is coming back and physical death will claim our lives, unless Jesus comes back before we die. Even still, Jesus' return and or our death are uncertain as to when they shall occur, thus, for both, His return and our death, we should always be prepared. The question before us is: "Will you be ready?"

As we examine the *Parable of the Ten Virgins*, once again Jesus highlights something familiar in order to communicate a spiritual truth. This, I stated in our previous chapter, is the method or technique of a *parable*. A *parable employs* the customary or ordinary as representative or symbolic of something else. In the case of today's *parable*, Jesus presents a slice of village life in Palestine. In the environment of His audience, the *Parable of the Wise and Foolish Virgins* is a real-life situation. Weddings were big in Palestine then, as they are now, and Jesus takes advantage of the joyous occasion of the wedding ceremony and its pending preparations in order to make clear the readiness required upon His return. Wedding customs differ from country to country and from culture to culture. Unlike what we may be acquainted with, in the Jewish custom the bridal party awaited the arrival of the bridegroom, while it is our custom to await the arrival of the bride. In the Jewish custom, when the bridegroom arrived, the bridal party was expected to be ready.

One feature of Jewish weddings at the time of Jesus could pose problems for us, which is the fact that weddings in those days were protracted. In other words, they were long and drawn out. The actual rite of marriage was one day, but the wedding took days, weeks, months and, sometimes, years. During this time the bride and groom lived apart, yet they were legally bound to each other, only disavowed through a bill of divorce. The point of protraction is what Jesus wanted to emphasize in order to illustrate the importance of being prepared to meet Him when He returns. Just as no one knew the arrival date or hour of the bridegroom, no one knows the re-arrival date or hour of Jesus

Christ. It is readiness that is underscored. It is readiness that is the point of the *parable*.

The *Parable of the Ten Virgins* is introduced to us as an extended lesson Jesus gives on 'faithful service.' In the closing verses of Chapter 24, Jesus talks about *stewardship* and the blessing that befalls upon stewards (servants) who are found faithful in the affairs of their lord's household. In essence, the *Parable of the Ten Virgins* is a spinoff of another parable of Jesus entitled, *the Parable of the Faithful Servant*. This parable is recorded in Matthew 24:42-51. It too emphasizes the need to be watchful of and ready for the Day of Jesus' return. Yet, it also stresses how important it is that we be found working while we wait—working on the things the Lord has given us to do.

As Christians, we are stewards in the Lord's household. A 'steward' manages the business of someone else. A 'steward' is appointed to supervise what belongs to another. I have stated over the years that, as a people of God, we have no business apart from God's business. In other words, our business is His business. We are expected to use what God has entrusted to us faithfully, on His behalf, until His Son comes again. The Apostle Paul tells us in 1st Corinthians 4:2, "*Moreover, it is required in stewards that a man be found faithful.*" The term "faithful" means 'loyal,' 'constant,' and 'steadfast.' It is faithfulness that makes us ready. It is faithfulness that prepares us for the Lord's return.

The *Parable of the Faithful Steward* (Servant) also teaches us that it is foolish of us to shirk our responsibilities as stewards, thinking the Lord's delay gives permission for unfaithfulness—thinking we could ignore the Lord's household affairs and indulge ourselves with the pleasures of this world. Such thinking, the *parable teaches,* is foolish, and such thinking, the *parable* also teaches, makes us guilty of negligent behavior. The military has a term for negligent behavior—it is called "Dereliction of duty," United States Code Title 10-892, Article 92, which applies to all branches of the US military. *Dereliction of duty* is a willful neglect to perform one's duties. It is an abandonment of obligation. It is a disregard of commitment. In such case, instead of blessing, there shall be curse and torment. In such case, Matthew 24:51 says, *"there shall be weeping and gnashing of teeth,"* as the "evil servant," who is the unfaithful servant, shall be given his or her allotment "with the hypocrites."

The point of both the *Parable of the Faithful Steward* and that of the *Ten Virgins* is; no one knows the return date but for certain the Lord is coming back. In the interval of *departure* and *return,* we should always be ready. Be ready! Be ready because though the *Landowner* and the *Bridegroom tarries,* the Landowner and the Bridegroom shall come. Jesus is both the *Landowner* and the *Bridegroom.* He is the One who has commissioned us. He is the One we are espoused to. Jesus is coming back. Will you be ready? Are you faithful while He's away? Are you working while He's away? Are you diligent while He's away? Are you prepared to meet Him?

In the *Parable of the Ten Virgins* the Bible says, *"Five of them were wise, and five were foolish"* (Matthew 25:2). *"Those who were foolish took their lamps,"* but *"took no oil,"* *"but the wise took oil in their vessels with their lamps"* (Matthew 25:3-4), and while *"the bridegroom was delayed, they all slumbered and slept"* (Matthew 25:5). Let me interject: it is okay to sleep, but make sure you are ready when awakened. Make sure you are ready for the day and the hour. Make sure you are ready for the moment of His arrival. Make sure you are ready when you hear the midnight cry. Make sure you are ready for the trumpet sound of God. Make sure your work is not undone. Make sure you are busy when Jesus comes. Make sure there is oil for your lamp. Be prepared at all times. Be prepared because we do not know when He will come. Be prepared because we do know that He will come. And when He comes, Jesus is coming back to receive those who are prepared. And when Jesus comes the door will then be shut, and the opportunity will then be lost. The question is: "Are you ready?" The question is: "Are you ready to meet the Lord?" The question is: "Are you ready to go in?

Forty days after resurrection Jesus went away, but Jesus is coming back! He went away to prepare a Place. And Jesus promised us He is coming back to receive us and to take us where He is (see John 14). The question again is: "Are you ready?" If not, get ready. Get busy. Be faithful. Be prepared at all times. Jesus is coming back! The songwriter says, "Be also ready" (Trinity All Nations Choir). Be also ready because we know not the day or the hour.

Be also ready because Jesus is coming back. It may be early. It may be late. It may be today, tomorrow, next week, or next year, but one day He is coming back. Jesus is coming back for His Bride for the *Marriage Supper of the Lamb*. Heaven is preparing, but *will you be ready*? Will you go in or be left out? Once the door is closed, it is closed. Late is too late. Prepare yourself right now. Get ready and stay ready every moment of every day, for one day it will be said, *the Bridegroom cometh!* WILL YOU BE READY?

CHAPTER 3
WILL IT BE "SERVANT WELL DONE?"

Parable of the Talents

Matthew 25:14-30

[14] "For the Kingdom of Heaven is like a man traveling to a far country, who called his own servants and delivered his goods to them. [15] And to one he gave five talents, to another two, and to another one, to each according to his own ability; and immediately he went on a journey. [16] Then he who had received the five talents went and traded with them, and made another five talents. [17] And likewise he who had received two gained two more also. [18] But he who had received one went and dug in the ground, and hid his lord's money. [19] After a long time the lord of those servants came and settled accounts with them. [20] "So he who had received five talents came and brought five other talents, saying, 'Lord, you delivered to me five talents; look, I have gained five more talents besides them.' [21] His lord said to him, 'Well done, good and faithful servant; you were faithful over a few things, I will make you ruler over

many things. Enter into the joy of your lord.' [22] He also who had received two talents came and said, 'Lord, you delivered to me two talents; look, I have gained two more talents besides them.' [23] His lord said to him, 'Well done, good and faithful servant; you have been faithful over a few things, I will make you ruler over many things. Enter into the joy of your lord.' [24] "Then he who had received the one talent came and said, 'Lord, I knew you to be a hard man, reaping where you have not sown, and gathering where you have not scattered seed. [25] And I was afraid, and went and hid your talent in the ground. Look, there you have what is yours.' [26] "But his lord answered and said to him, 'You wicked and lazy servant, you knew that I reap where I have not sown, and gather where I have not scattered seed. [27] So you ought to have deposited my money with the bankers, and at my coming I would have received back my own with interest. [28] Therefore take the talent from him, and give it to him who has ten talents. [29] 'For to everyone who has, more will be given, and he will have abundance; but from him who does not have, even what he has will be taken away. [30] And cast the unprofitable servant into the outer darkness. There will be weeping and gnashing of teeth."

As we continue our series on The Stories Jesus Told, once again we examine one of the parables Jesus uttered during the final days of His earthly ministry. In the last two chapters we analyzed the two other parables from the 25th Chapter of

Matthew's Gospel, as well as one other from the 24th Chapter. All three of those, the Parable of the Faithful Steward, the Parable of the Ten Virgins, and the Parable of the Sheep and the Goats, as well as this one deal with the Second Coming of Christ and the judgment that will ensue once He comes, and how best to prepare ourselves for the Day we must all stand before Him and give an account of how well, or not, we've been faithful, or not, with the divine resources of time, talent, and treasure. Time, talent and treasure are priceless commodities entrusted to us by God. God expects us to use each wisely in rendering to Him a return on His investment when His Son returns to collect. This, in essence, is the primary thesis of today's parable. It is aptly called *The Parable of the Talents* because it highlights a distribution of talents. The term "talent," as it relates to Matthew 25:14-30, was a unit of weight applied to precious metals, such as *gold* and *silver*. *Talent*, as it relates to Matthew 25:14-30, was *currency or money*. In fact *talent*, as it relates to our text, was a lot of money that was handed over to three servants in proportion to their ability.

Like us, each of the servants in the story did not have the same aptitude, skill, gift, or proclivity; however, like us, each was given something by their lord to increase it above what they were given. Like us, all were not expected to produce the same amount; however, like us, each were to use what they were given to the benefit of the giver. One lesson we can readily glean from the parable is that God does not demand of us equal results, but He does expect from each of us a level of effort in accordance with our abilities. I repeat: God does not demand of us equal results, but He does expect from each of us a level of effort in accordance with our abilities. Again, we all do not have the same abilities, nor do we all have the same gifts. Still, God has endowed each of us with Kingdom resources that He wants us to employ or utilize in favor of the Kingdom. This is why the parable begins by saying, *"For the Kingdom of Heaven is like a man traveling to a far country, who called his own servants and delivered unto them his goods"* (Matthew 25:14).

I stated in the very first chapter, *The 'Right Side' is the Right Side*, that Jesus shared stories such as this story to help people understand what the Kingdom of God is like and what is expected of those of us who are citizens of His Kingdom. By way of clarification, if you are a Christian you have citizenship in God's Kingdom. As a citizen, God has expectations of you that are catalogued in the citizen's manual, which is the Word of God—the Holy Scriptures—the Bible that contains 66 books of instructions. God wants us to be aware of what is required of us, thus the requirements are recorded and illustrated for us throughout Scripture. The requirements are made even easier to understand in the parables of Jesus. This is why Jesus says, *"For the Kingdom of Heaven is like."* Through parable, He seeks to instruct all who follow Him of what is anticipated of us while He is away, and of what awaits us when He returns.

When you look at Matthew 25:14-30, the very first word is "For." Its placement, as the first word, is here to attach verse fourteen and the parable to the previous verse and parable warning that the return of Jesus will be sudden and unannounced. The previous parable is *The Parable of the Ten Virgins*, which we expounded on in the last chapter. Verse thirteen says: *"Watch therefore, for ye know neither the day nor the hour wherein the Son of man cometh"* (Matthew 25:13). The *Parable of the Talents* is designed to highlight the roles and responsibilities that are assigned to us as disciples of Christ. It also underscores the judgment we will face when Jesus returns, based upon the service we render as *stewards* in His absence. In the second chapter, *Will You Be Ready*, we defined a 'steward' as "someone who manages the affairs of someone else." We said that "a steward is simply appointed to supervise [or conduct the operations] of what belongs to another."

In the *Parable of the Talents*, three individuals were entrusted with a large sum of money. The money was but a tool to gauge their faithfulness, as money is also a tool to gauge ours. In the parable, the money was but a tool with which each were to work in relation to ability and opportunity, as it is also for us. With money and through money God measures our character, heart, sensibility, and reliability. Bible readers know that Jesus says, *"For where your treasure is, there will your heart be also"* (Matthew 6:21). It is through our use of money that God determines who He can trust with even more. How we manage money, time, and our God provided gifts and abilities will determine whether we will hear Him say *servant well done* or *wicked and slothful servant*. The parable teaches us that God is watching what we do with the opportunities we have. Earlier, I stated that each of the three servants in the parable did not have the same aptitude, skill, gift, or proclivity. Despite the difference in their individual aptitude, skill, gift, and proclivity, each had an opportunity to produce something with what they had. So do we. We will please or displease God depending on how we make use of our opportunities. God does not waste His resources nor does He excuse laziness. *Laziness* is the trait of someone who is unwilling to work. It is the attribute of someone who is unenthusiastic about work and disinclined to work. *Laziness* upsets God because *laziness* is counterproductive to all that is God, as well as to all that God expects 'of' us and 'from' us. The Bible says, in Proverbs 18:9, *"A lazy person is as bad as someone who destroys things"* (NLT). Never forget that God does not invest in us time, talent, or treasure for us to be unproductive, fruitless, uncreative, and lazy. Always remember that God expects to receive from us 'increase' from what He invested in us. When God looks at what He receives from us, compared to what He gave us, the question is: "Will it be servant, well done?"

In returning to the parable; *"unto one he gave five talents, to another two, and to another one."* In this some may ask, "Why the difference?" This is a good question. Among the servants in the parable, as well as among us, there is a variation of allocation because God knows each of us better than we know ourselves. He knows our capacity to carry out an assignment. God knows that some of us can do more with *more*, and He knows that with some of us, *less* is just right. So with this knowledge, the provision is disbursed according to *competency* or *capability*. But always remember, though the disbursements vary, God looks to see from each of us activity and supplement. *Supplement* means 'in addition to,' 'extra,' 'more,' and 'bonus.'

In the parable, three servants are enough to accentuate Jesus' purpose and point. These three provide adequate samples to typify the variety of persons involved in the Lord's business between the time frame of His departure and return. Among these three I am included and among these three you are included. In fact, in these three are depictions of every follower of Christ from His giving of the Great Commission to His reappearance to judge our dutifulness to it. The Great Commission says, *"Go ye therefore and make disciples of all nations; baptize them in the Name of the Father and of the Son and of the Holy Spirit; teach them to observe all things I have commanded you"* (Matthew 28:19-20). Again, the question is: "Will it be servant well done?" Put another way: "Will it be *well done, thou good and faithful servant?"*

In the parable, the one who was given five talents worked his five into ten, and to him it was said, "Well done." In the parable, the one who was given two talents worked his two into four, and to him it was said, "Well done." And then it came to the one who was given one. He neither worked it nor produced anything more than what was given, and to him it was not said, "Servant, well done," but to him his lord pronounced, *"Thou wicked and slothful servant,"* you knew what was expected, but did nothing to achieve it. Thus, what he had was taken away and then given to someone else—to someone else who had been faithful—to someone else who did something—to someone else who pleased his lord—to someone else more deserving. We must produce or lose. We must produce or die.

If you want to hear the Lord say *"Servant, well done,"* then get busy in the Father's Will and be diligent with His gifts. Be diligent with His time. Be diligent with His talent. Be diligent with His treasure. Be found faithful as a steward. If you want to hear the Lord say *"Servant, well done,"* then do not hide what God gave you, and do not suppress what God gave you, and do not withhold what God gave you, but work what you have. Work while it is day. Work while you can. Work while He is away, for one day He is coming back. And when Jesus comes back, He will promote. And when Jesus comes back, He will demote. And when Jesus comes back, He will reward. And when Jesus comes back, He will penalize. At that time Jesus will separate the *sheep* from the *goats* and the *wise* from the *foolish*. The question is: "Will it be *servant, well done?*" Will you enter into His joy or be banished from His sight? Will you gain or will you lose? Are you a *have* or *have-not?* What will it be? What will the Lord say to you when you stand before Him? What will the Lord do to you when you stand before Him? Produce or lose. Produce or die.

When Jesus comes back, work will be rewarded. Excuses will be rejected. Work will be praised. Excuses will be punished. Workers will go in. Excusers will be shut out. What will the Lord say to you? What will the Lord do to you? I hear a song in my ear: "If when you give the best of your service, telling the world the Savior's come; be not dismayed when men don't believe you, He'll understand and say well done" (*He'll Understand and Say Well Done*, Lucie Eddie Campbell). I hear another song in my ear: "Our talents may be few, these may be small, but unto Him is due our best, our all" (*Our Best*, Salathiel C. Kirk). I want to hear Jesus say "Well done!" What about you? Well done faithful servant? Well done loyal servant? Well done devoted servant? WELL DONE! WELL DONE! WELL DONE! WELL DONE!

Chapter 4

How Often Should We Forgive?

Parable of the Unforgiving Servant

Matthew 18:21-35

[21] Then Peter came to Him and said, "Lord, how often shall my brother sin against me, and I forgive him? Up to seven times?" [22] Jesus said to him, "I do not say to you, up to seven times, but up to seventy times seven. [23] Therefore the Kingdom of Heaven is like a certain king who wanted to settle accounts with his servants. [24] And when he had begun to settle accounts, one was brought to him who owed him ten thousand talents. [25] But as he was not able to pay, his master commanded that he be sold, with his wife and children and all that he had, and that payment be made. [26] The servant therefore fell down before him, saying, 'Master, have patience with me, and I will pay you all.' [27] Then the master of that servant was moved with compassion, released him, and forgave him the debt. [28] "But that servant went out and found one of his fellow servants who owed him a hundred denarii; and he laid hands on him and

took him by the throat, saying, 'Pay me what you owe!' [29] So his fellow servant fell down at his feet and begged him, saying, 'Have patience with me, and I will pay you all.' [30] And he would not, but went and threw him into prison till he should pay the debt. [31] So when his fellow servants saw what had been done, they were very grieved, and came and told their master all that had been done. [32] Then his master, after he had called him, said to him, 'You wicked servant! I forgave you all that debt because you begged me. [33] Should you not also have had compassion on your fellow servant, just as I had pity on you?' [34] And his master was angry, and delivered him to the torturers until he should pay all that was due to him. [35] "So My heavenly Father also will do to you if each of you, from his heart, does not forgive his brother his trespasses."

The question of our subject has it foundation in another parable of Jesus. This parable is entitled *The Parable of the Unforgiving Servant*. It has to do with the subject of 'forgiveness' and deliberates the question of *how often should we forgive* people who wrong us. This is a question, no doubt, many of us have asked ourselves. It is a question that was asked of Jesus within Matthew 18:21-35 by one of His disciples. In fact, it is this question of *how often we should forgive* that initiates the parable, and through parable we are allowed to hear the response of Jesus. Again, a *parable* is simply a story that is told in order to communicate a spiritual principle.

The *Parable of the Unforgiving Servant teaches* us that God's forgiveness and human forgiveness are innately related. In other words, both are intertwined with each other, knotted together, two sides of one coin, and distinctively inseparable. The parable teaches us that it is essential to forgive, especially in recognition and appreciation of how we have been forgiven by God. It highlights the ramifications of unforgiveness, as it also underscores the magnitude of God's grace toward us. *Forgiveness* is no doubt the counsel of Matthew 18:21-35, but still the question remains: "How often should we forgive?" In Matthew 18:21-35 we are eavesdropping on a conversation between Jesus and His disciples. However, one of the problems with eavesdropping is that oftentimes we miss something, and what is missed, many times, is critical to a proper analysis of the *what* and *why*. What is heard in Matthew 18:21-35 is not the whole conversation between Jesus and His disciples because we are snooping midpoint. In order to get the complete discussion and why the question was asked of Jesus concerning the quantity of forgiveness, we need examine the wider conversation.

Prior to Matthew 18:21-35, Jesus has been talking about humility, accountability, reconciliation, and restoration, and how best the church should handle members of the church when they have faults—one with another. It was Jesus' discourse on dealing with a sinning brother, verses 15 through 20, that prompts Peter to approach Jesus with the question, *"Lord, how often shall my brother sin against me, and I forgive him?"* How often? Many of us have pondered the same question, as well as asked it of others.

How often? How often must we exonerate the wrongs of others? How often must we turn the other cheek? How often must we go the extra mile? How many times do we have to cry? How many times do we have to hurt? How many times must we hold our peace? How many times must we refuse to retaliate? I think the question Peter asked was a human question: *how often should we forgive?* In asking the question, Peter also supplies a number he thought would garner the approval of Jesus. Prior to the question Peter had done his math. He says, *"Lord, how many times must I forgive,"* is it *"up to seven times?"* Peter says *seven* because, based on Jewish tradition, you could forgive three times, but not four, which was probably a misreading or misinterpretation of the Book of the Prophet Amos, in particular the first chapter, where it was understood that God only forgives three times for the same offence. So thinking himself gracious, Peter takes the number three, multiplies it by two, and then he adds one, coming up with seven. The number seven is the number of completeness and perfection.

Seven is a significant number in the framework of the Bible. In six days God created all that is and on the seventh day He rested. The Bible as a whole was originally divided into seven major divisions: The Law, the Prophets, the Writings or the Psalms, the Gospel and Acts, the General Epistles, the Epistles of Paul, and the Book of Revelation. In the Book of Revelation there are seven letters to seven churches, seven candlesticks, seven spirits, seven stars, seven seals, seven trumpets, seven vials, seven dooms, and seven new things. In the Book of Hebrews there are seven titles for Christ: Heir of All Things, Captain of our Salvation, Apostle, Author of Salvation, Forerunner, High Priest, and the Author and Finisher of our Faith. Seven days complete a week, and there are seven annual holy days among the Jews. These are but a few examples of the significance of seven. Peter says, not three, but seven. Surely, who could ask for more than this? But to his surprise or dismay, Jesus gives another number, which is not a number, but a statement against limitation. Instead of seven times, Jesus says *"up to seventy times seven,"* which according to mathematical standards is '490,' but according to Jesus, *seventy times seven equals* infinity. It means 'no limit.' It means 'as often as they offend you, you forgive.' And to get His point across Jesus shares the *Parable of the Unforgiving Servant*. He begins it by saying: *"The Kingdom of Heaven is like a king who wanted to settle his accounts with his servants."* Thus, he began to work through the accounts one by one, and as he was working through the accounts a servant was brought to him who owed him ten thousand talents. A *talent*, I stated in the last chapter, was a unit of weight applied to precious metals, such as *gold* and *silver*. I said it was *currency* or *money* and a lot of it, and in the previous chapter I only examined *five* talents, *two* talents, and *one* talent, but in this chapter the amount is *ten thousand*.

Ten thousand talents was the equivalent, some say, anywhere from 15 years to 3,000 years of labor wages. By either standard this was an enormous amount of debt, and one may wonder what this servant did to accumulate such a huge debt. His debt represents the debt we owed God, before Calvary, because of sin. It was, as the servant's debt, beyond human ability to repay. It was, as the servant's debt, a hopeless situation. But God! Ephesians 2:4 declares *"But God, who is rich in mercy."* As the servant was called before the king he was asked to settle up a debt he could not repay, and like us with God, he falls to his knees and appeals for mercy. Like us with God he asked for grace. Like us with God he pleads for patience. And like God with us, being moved with compassion, the servant was granted clemency. His debt was cancelled, and like us, the servant was set free. But no sooner than he was freed, like many of us, we are told, *"That servant went out and found one of his fellow servants who owed him a hundred denarii."* He went out looking. He went out searching. He went out on a mission to find one who owed him something. Let us understand, a hundred denarii was about 100 days wages; nothing compared to the 15 to 3,000 years of debt he was forgiven. We are told, *"He laid hands on him and took him by the throat, saying, 'Pay me what you owe.'"* When you examine Matthew 18:21-35 the servant, who had been forgiven, refused to forgive, although what was expressed to him were the very words he had expressed to the king. *"His fellow servant fell down at his feet and begged him, saying, 'Have patience with me, and I will pay you all.'"* But we are told, like some of us, *"He would not,"* and did to him what was not done to himself. His debt was forgiven, but he refused to forgive. A n d because of his refusal to forgive he lost his own forgiveness. Other servants reported what he had done and the king recalled him before his court, reprimanded him, and called him *wicked*. He was called wicked because what flowed to him did not flow through him. The king said, *"I forgave you all that debt [simply] because you begged me." "Should you not have also had compassion on your fellow servant, as I had pity on you?" "His master was angry, and delivered him to the torturers until he should pay all that was due to him."* The Bible says *"Be not deceived; God is not mocked: for whatsoever a man soweth, that shall he also reap"* (Galatians 6:7). Jesus sums up the parable by saying, *"So My Heavenly Father will also do to each of you, if, from your heart, you do not forgive."* So, *how often should we forgive?*

We should forgive as often as we need forgiveness, and if the truth be told, we need forgiveness often. Often, we need the grace of God. Often, we need the patience of God. Often, we need the mercy of God. Often, we need to be pardoned by God. The question is: *How often should we forgive?* As God forgives us we should forgive, and as many times as God forgives us we should forgive. God's forgiveness has no boundary. It is immeasurable. It cannot be calculated. The Bible says, *"The LORD's love never ends; His mercies never stop. They are new every morning"* (Lamentations 3:22-23, NCV). So, *how often should we forgive?* The Kingdom way is without number. The Kingdom way has no limit. If you desire the forgiveness of God, then you must be willing to forgive. In Matthew 6:14-15 Jesus says, and I paraphrase: 'If you forgive, God forgives, but if not, God does not.' In forgiveness, we align ourselves with God. Through forgiveness, we demonstrate the heart of God. So, *how often should we forgive?*

When you appreciate what God has done you pass it on. Real *forgiveness* is not based on formula or law, but it is rooted in experience. We are forgiven to forgive. We are set free to set free. What flows to us must flow through us. The Bible says, *"Forgive one another, just as God through Christ has forgiven you"* (Ephesians 4:32, NLT). It matters not the situation. It matters not the circumstance. The God way is forgiveness. The God way is compassion. The God way is release. The God way is unconditional. This is the nature of God and what is expected of us. As God forgives, so must we. We must likewise do the same. Forgive those who have wronged you. Forgive those who have hurt you. Forgive those who disappoint you. Forgive those who have caused you pain. Forgive every lie. Forgive the indignation. Forgive the harassment. Forgive the indiscretion. Free yourself so you can live by letting go of the past. What is done has been done. Forgive and move forward. Let it go and let them go. God has a future for your life. But you cannot embrace the future holding on and looking back: DELETE, DEFRIEND, DISCONNECT, and FORGIVE. *Forgiveness* is the way of living life to its fullest. *Forgiveness* is the way you break every chain. Forgiveness is how you pull down the strongholds, and overcome the obstacles. *How often should we forgive?*

As followers of Jesus Christ, the way we deal with others is how God deals with us. God forgives us, and God restarts us, and

God gives us another chance. He gives us a second chance. He gives us a third chance. He gives us a fourth chance. He gives us a fifth chance. God has given us unlimited chances with all the sin we have committed and all the debt we owe. His grace transformed us and His mercy revived us. God's patience assisted us and His compassion forgave us. *How often should we forgive?* It is how often we have been forgiven and how often God still forgives. And when I think about how many times that the LORD has forgiven me, I lose count. God forgives, and He forgives, and He forgives, and He forgives. And like God we must forgive, and forgive, and forgive, and forgive. We do not condone. We do not approve of. We do not excuse, but release ourselves so we can be ourselves. Let it go. Let it go. Let it go. Let it go. How many times? We do it as often as it takes. LET IT GO!

Chapter 5

Lost But Loved

Parable of the Prodigal Son

Luke 15:11-24

[11]Then He said: "A certain man had two sons. [12] And the younger of them said to his father, 'Father, give me the portion of goods that falls to me.' So he divided to them his livelihood. [13]And not many days after, the younger son gathered all together, journeyed to a far country, and there wasted his possessions with prodigal living. [14] But when he had spent all, there arose a severe famine in that land and he began to be in want. [15] Then he went and joined himself to a citizen of that country, and he sent him into his fields to feed swine. [16] And he would gladly have filled his stomach with the pods that the swine ate, and no one gave him anything. [17] "But when he came to himself, he said, 'How many of my father's hired servants have bread enough and to spare, and I perish with hunger! [18] I will arise and go to my father, and will say to him, "Father, I have sinned against Heaven and before you, [19] and

I am no longer worthy to be called your son. Make me like one of your hired servants.'" [20] "And he arose and came to his father. But when he was still a great way off, his father saw him and had compassion, and ran and fell on his neck and kissed him. [21] And the son said to him, 'Father, I have sinned against Heaven and in your sight, and am no longer worthy to be called your son.' [22] "But the father said to his servants, 'Bring out the best robe and put it on him, and put a ring on his hand and sandals on his feet. [23] And bring the fatted calf here and kill it, and let us eat and be merry; [24] for this my son was dead and is alive again; he was lost and is found.' And they began to be merry.

Once again, by way of parable, we are granted the privilege of hearing Jesus clarify the emphasis of Heaven here on earth. We also glean instruction from Jesus, through story form, regarding the mandate of God for His people. I have stated throughout that Jesus used parables to communicate a spiritual principle employing graphic analogies utilizing common things or situations that were familiar to His audience of hearers. Jesus also used parables to distinguish sincere seekers from those whose motives were disingenuous or deceitful. *Parables* required more explanation, and explanation was only given to His disciples that they may see and perceive, as well as hear and understand. At one point in His ministry Jesus taught exclusively in parable (see Matthew 13:34). *Parables* were easily remembered, the characters were bold, and the symbolism was rich in meaning. The parable before us is the *Parable of the Prodigal Son* and, like many of the other parables of Jesus; it is the byproduct of controversy. In this case, what prompts Jesus into parable mode is an accusation that was leveled against Him by the *Pharisees and scribes*.

The *Pharisees* and *scribes* were two of the three major religious groups during the time of our text—the other group was the *Sadducees*. These three, along with the *elders*, the *chief priests*, and the *high priest* comprised the *Sanhedrin Council*, which was the supreme religious body at the time of Jesus. It was the Sanhedrin Council that assembled in haste to judge Jesus, and the same Council that condemned Jesus to the Cross. *Scribes and Pharisees* opposed Jesus throughout His ministry. They constantly sought ways to find loopholes in His teachings and actions that would grant them opportunity to disparage what Jesus said **or** did, especially in public in front of the crowds that thronged Him. *Scribes* had knowledge of the law and could draft legal documents, such as contracts for marriage, divorce, loans, inheritance, the sale of land, etc. At the time of this story every village had at least one scribe, and some scribes were also Pharisees. *Pharisees* were members of a faction that believed in resurrection and in following legal traditions that were ascribed, not to the Scriptures, but to "the traditions of men." Like the scribes, the Pharisees were also well-known legal experts. Hence, the partial overlap of membership between *scribes and Pharisees*.

Within the context of Luke 15:11-24, it was the *Pharisees and scribes* who whispered among themselves charging Jesus with consorting with sinners (see verse 2). Interjected lesson: no matter what you do there will always be whisperers. No matter what you do there will always be faultfinders. No matter what you do there will always be critics. No matter what you do there will always be people who complain and nitpick about all that you do. The *Pharisees and scribes* protested that Jesus consorted with sinners. *Consort* means to "habitually associate with someone that is disapproved of by others." The *Pharisees and scribes* frowned upon Jesus because he congregated with individuals they deemed despicable and repulsive, and as people who were alienated from God because of lifestyle or occupation. It was the viewpoint of the *Pharisees and scribes* that these who drew near to hear Jesus, "tax-collectors" and "sinners," were unrighteous degenerates unworthy of attention, let alone, association. In their judgment, these were 'they' that no respectable Jew would have anything to do with. Therefore, if Jesus embraced their company, then surely Jesus was equally unclean and immoral. So they grumbled saying, *"This man receives sinners and eats with them"* (Luke 15:2). Let us park here for another lesson. Be careful how you judge people based upon the people around them. It is not always "guilty by association." This is true in some cases, but not necessarily in all. In Matthew 9:12 Jesus says, *"It is not the healthy who need a doctor, but the sick"* (NIV). Jesus came here for sick people. Jesus came here for sinners. Jesus came here for tax-collectors, and prostitutes, and drunkards, and thieves—for the lame, sick, deaf, diseased, and dumb. He came for the ostracized. He came for the demoralized. He came for the outcast. Jesus came for those who are rejected by others. He said, *"For the Son of man is come to seek and to save that which was lost"* (Luke 19:10). If the truth be told, at one time or another we all were lost. At one time or another we all were outsiders. At one time or another we all were prodigals. At one time or another we all were sinners.

Those who came near to hear Jesus were those Jesus came here to be near. Yes they were lost, but in the Father's heart they were treasured souls. So in reply to the criticism against Him, Jesus responds by way of parable. In fact, Jesus gives us three parables: the *Parable of the Lost Sheep* (verses 4-7), the *Parable of the Lost Coin* (verses 8-10), and the parable of our text, known as the *Parable of the Prodigal Son,* or the *Parable of the Lost Son* (verses 11-24). All three present a picture of the value God places on the lost. All three illustrate the magnitude of God's love for the lost. All three underscore the joy of Heaven when what was lost is found.

The entire 15th Chapter of Luke is a deposition on God's heart for the lost—the 'lost' being sinners of every kind. It highlights the fact that God loves people regardless of the sin, as well as the fact that each life, no matter the color, gender, culture, locality, or social class is significant to God. This includes you and this includes me. *"For God so loved the world that He gave His only Begotten Son, that whosoever believes in Him should not perish, but have everlasting life"* (John 3:16). Luke 15 illuminates God's zeal for salvation and it spells out how important one soul is to God. In this chapter we have three stories, but one central and unifying message. It is one message from three different angles, all pronouncing *"there is joy in Heaven over one sinner who repents"* (Luke 15:7, 10). This message is resounded in the *Parable of the Lost Sheep*, amplified in the *Parable of the Lost Coin*, and reinforced and solidified within the *Parable of the Lost Son*.

In the story of the lost sheep, a shepherd has 100 sheep. One wanders astray, but the shepherd leaves the 99 in search of the one, and when he finds it, he lays the one on his shoulders and rejoices. Upon his return, he calls together his *friends* and *neighbors* for celebration of recovery. The point is: Lost, but not discarded. God loves strayaways! In the story of the lost coin, a woman has 10 silver coins but loses one inside of her house. She lights a lamp, sweeps the house, and searches carefully until she finds it. We are told that when she has found it, *"she calls her friends and neighbors together, saying, 'Rejoice with me, for I have found the piece which I lost'"* (v. 9)! The point is: Even if a thing is lost on the inside, it is still worthy of a search—in the story of the lost son, *"A certain man had two sons"* (v. 11). We are informed that the younger demands of his father his share of inheritance. He says to his father, *"Give me the portion of goods that falls to me"* (v. 12). Technically, he had nothing coming. The father was not dead. Nevertheless, the father divides the inheritance between his sons, then, *"Not many days after, the younger son gathered all together, journeyed to a far country, and there wasted his possessions with prodigal living"* (v. 13). The term 'prodigal' means "wastefully extravagant." It describes a lifestyle that is reckless in spending and irresponsible in character. It describes a lifestyle that is sinful, vile, careless, and foolish. This young man, like many of us, did things he should not have done. He lived an unrestricted life on his father's money until all the money was gone. He saved none of it. He spent all of it. He, no doubt, partied. He, no doubt, drank a lot. He, no doubt, smoked dope and bought sex—he *wasted his possessions with prodigal living*. And like some of us, he had no thought of the future and made no preparations for the future. He wasted everything that he had. Everything he was given. Everything the father worked for. We are told in the story that, *"When he had spent all, there arose a severe famine in that land and he began to be in want"* (v. 14). *Famine* means shortage. With no money and no food, *"he joined himself to a citizen of that country"* (v. 15), who sent him to feed swine. *Swine* is another term for "hogs" and "pigs." To a Jew this was a disgraceful place to be—feeding swine with a desire to eat pig food.

You may like pig food: ribs, pork chops, ham and bacon, but pig food is not kosher in the Jewish diet. However, this is where the prodigal son found himself because *"no one gave him anything"* (v. 16). In other words, no one helped him out. Like many of us, once his money was gone he was alone. But thank God *"he came to himself"* (v. 17). Here is another lesson: You cannot be saved unless you come to yourself. You cannot be found unless you come to yourself. When *he came to himself* it means he considered his life. At one time he was caught up in himself, but now he looks at himself and realizes how foolish he had been. Have you ever looked back over your life at the foolish things you have done?

In looking at himself, the prodigal son questions himself. He considers his situation and the blessings of his father's house. He says, *"How many of my father's hired servants have bread enough and to spare, and I perish with hunger"* (v. 17)! I will arise and go home. I will tell my father, *"I have sinned against Heaven and before you"* (v. 18). I am no longer worthy to be called 'son.' Make me like your servants. So, *he came to himself* and went home, but he went home humbled and with a repentant heart, which is all God wants from us. God desires 'a broken and contrite spirit.' God wants confession. God wants self-examination. God wants apology. God wants a *Psalm 51* prayer. Always remember: we may be lost, but God loves us. God loves us in spite of. God loves us no matter what. No matter what the sin or situation. God will forgive and accept us, and He receives us with open arms. This is the moral to the story. This is the point of the parables.

Jesus came here to retrieve. Jesus came here to recover. Jesus came here to search out. Jesus came here to restore. He came for the lost. He came for the backslider. He came for the wayward. He came for the prodigal. Jesus came to demonstrate the heart of His Father. God loves us. God cares for us. God values us, and has a place for us in His Kingdom. But we must come to ourselves and acknowledge our sinful ways. We must say to God "Lord, I'm sorry." We must say to God "Lord, forgive me." We must say to God "Lord, clean me up." We must say to God "Lord, make me whole." The Bible says, *"Humble yourselves in the sight of the Lord, and He will lift you up"* (James 4:10). Humility gets the robe. Humility gets the ring. Humility gets the sandals. Humility gets a homecoming celebration. God says, "Come home." All you have to do is come to yourself. What God has is far better than anything else. You may be lost, but you are loved! You may be lost, but you are valued! You may be lost, but you are important! YOU ARE ALWAYS IN GOD'S HEART!

CHAPTER 6

WHO IS MY NEIGHBOR?
Parable of the Good Samaritan

Luke 10:25-37

²⁵ And behold, a certain lawyer stood up and tested Him, saying, "Teacher, what shall I do to inherit eternal life?" ²⁶ He said to him, "What is written in the law? What is your reading of it?" ²⁷ So he answered and said, "'you shall love the LORD your God with all your heart, with all your soul, with all your strength, and with all your mind,' and 'your neighbor as yourself.'" ²⁸ And He said to him, "You have answered rightly; do this and you will live." ²⁹ But he, wanting to justify himself, said to Jesus, "And who is my neighbor?" ³⁰ Then Jesus answered and said: "A certain man went down from Jerusalem to Jericho, and fell among thieves, who stripped him of his clothing, wounded him, and departed, leaving him half dead. ³¹ Now by chance a certain priest came down that road. And when he saw him, he passed by on the other side. ³² Likewise a Levite, when he arrived at the place, came and looked, and

passed by on the other side. 33 But a certain Samaritan, as he journeyed, came where he was. And when he saw him, he had compassion. 34 So he went to him and bandaged his wounds, pouring on oil and wine; and he set him on his own animal, brought him to an inn, and took care of him. 35 On the next day, when he departed, he took out two denarii, gave them to the innkeeper, and said to him, 'Take care of him; and whatever more you spend, when I come again, I will repay you.' 36 So which of these three do you think was neighbor to him who fell among the thieves?" 37 And he said, "He who showed mercy on him." Then Jesus said to him, "Go and do likewise."

A mong the parables of Jesus, the one of Luke 10:25-37 is thought to be the most recognizable and proverbial of them all. It is aptly called *The Parable of the Good Samaritan*. As in the case of many of His parables, it too is precipitated by yet another question posed to Jesus. In fact, it was two questions asked of Jesus that generates this moralistic story from Jesus. Both questions were initiated by an inquiry from "a certain lawyer," who the text says, *"stood up and tested Him"* (v. 25). For understanding, this "certain lawyer" was not the kind of lawyer who goes to court in a civil or criminal case. Instead, he was an expert in Mosaic Law. Some theologians interpret him to be a *Scribe*.

I mentioned in the last chapter that *Scribes* were among the three major religious groups that opposed Jesus. The other two are the *Pharisees* and *Sadducees*. *Scribes*, I said, had knowledge of the Law and could draft legal documents, such as contracts for marriage, divorce, loans, inheritance, the sale of land, etc. Thus, this lawyer, or scribe, was profoundly proficient in what Old Testament Scripture taught was mankind's duty to God, as well as mankind's duty to mankind. Having a thorough knowledge of the Law, his question to Jesus, therefore, was an inquisition to see what Jesus saw as the essential requirements of the Law. He says to Jesus, *"Teacher, what shall I do to inherit eternal life"* (v. 25), and on the surface the question appears to be a sincere one. An examination of the question affords us insight to where the lawyer's heart was spiritually. In his question he makes an assumption that something must be done in order to obtain eternal life. However, this assumption contradicts what salvation necessitates. The requisite of salvation is simply *faith*. In fact, we are taught through Scripture that salvation is a matter of *"grace through faith"* (see Ephesians 2:8-9). It has nothing to do with 'deeds' or 'works.' According to Romans 10:9, a person is saved through *confession* (by mouth) and *belief* (within the heart). The question was not a bad question, although Jesus knew the motive was disingenuous. *Disingenuous* means 'dishonest,' 'insincere,' 'hypocritical,' and 'deceitful.' Jesus could have used it as an opportunity to teach a lesson on salvation, but He chose rather to teach one on what it means to love both *God* and *neighbor*.

I love how Jesus employs what is called the 'Socratic Method.' This method responds to a question with a question. Often Jesus did this when approached by individuals with an agenda designed to disparage His ministry and message. In response to the question of *"What shall I do to inherit eternal life"* (v. 25), Jesus posed two of His own. One was *"What is written in the Law"* (v. 26), and the other, *"What is your reading of it"* (v. 26)? In other words, what is your understanding of what is written in the Law? By referring to the Law, Jesus directs the man to an authority they both acknowledge as truth. In this, Jesus avoids a conflict and places Himself in the position of evaluating the lawyer's answer, instead of the lawyer evaluating His.

In reply to the questions of Jesus, Deuteronomy 6:5 and Leviticus 19:18 are quoted: *"You shall love the LORD your God with all your heart, with all your soul, with all your strength and with all your mind"* (Deuteronomy), and love *"your neighbor as yourself"* (Leviticus). These Jesus taught as the greatest commandments (see Matthew 22:35-40). An implementation of these two fulfills the obligations of all. So Jesus says, *"You have answered rightly; do this and you will live"* (v. 28). But desiring to justify himself Jesus is asked, *"And who is my neighbor"* (v. 29). It is this question that initiates the *Parable of the Good Samaritan* (vv. 30-35):

> A certain man went down from Jerusalem to Jericho, and fell among thieves, who stripped him of his clothing, wounded him, and departed, leaving him half dead. Now by chance a certain priest came down that road. And when he saw him, he passed by on the other side. Likewise a Levite, when he arrived at the place, came and looked, and passed by on the other side. But a certain Samaritan, as he journeyed, came where he was. And when he saw him, he had compassion. So he went

to him and bandaged his wounds, pouring on oil and wine; and he set him on his own animal, brought him to an inn, and took care of him. On the next day, when he departed, he took out two denarii, gave them to the innkeeper, and said to him, 'Take care of him; and whatever more you spend, when I come again, I will repay you.'

Once He finished the story, Jesus turns to the lawyer with one more question: *"So which of these three* [Priest, Levite, or Samaritan] *do you think was neighbor to him who fell among the thieves"* (v. 36)? The answer: *"He who showed mercy on him"* (v. 37). The final word from Jesus: *"Go and do likewise"* (v. 37).

This story is told by Jesus in such a way that it is clear 'who is the neighbor.' He tells it as an indictment against the religious leaders and their abhorrence of who Jesus reached out to. Jesus reached out to *publicans* and *sinners*, who were deemed by the religious leaders unworthy of love and compassion, and as I stated in the last chapter, attention and association. The story is also aimed at the prejudice which the Jews had toward Samaritans. This is why Jesus utilizes one they despised as the champion of the parable. The question of *"And who is my neighbor"* (v. 29) was asked to regulate the Law's command to love by limiting the parameters of *who is my neighbor?* In the Greek language the term *neighbor* means "someone who is near." In Hebrew it means, "someone that you have an association with." These definitions interpret the expression with boundaries, giving us a sense as to who the Jews considered their neighbors. For Jews, only fellow Jews were neighbors. All others (Samaritans, Romans, and Foreigners) were excluded. Jesus gives us the *Parable of the Good Samaritan* to illustrate the Kingdom's classification of *neighbor*. In this, the question of neighbor is answered.

The *Parable of the Good Samaritan* tells the story of a man traveling from Jerusalem to Jericho and while traveling he is robbed of everything he had. His clothes are taken. He is beaten, and left on the road "half dead" (see verse 30). Historians tell us that the road from Jerusalem to Jericho was a dangerous road, often inhabited by thieves and robbers. It was on this road, while a man struggled for life, that a priest happens by, and instead of helping him, he passes by on the other side. If anyone would have known God's law of love, it was this priest; however, his lack of action teaches us that *knowledge alone is not sufficient*. Love demands involvement. Love requires action. But like some of us, the priest looks and does nothing. Like some of us, he simply leaves the scene without involvement. Jesus spends no time describing him, but highlights his failure to show compassion. The action of the Levite is no better. He too does nothing. Like the priest, he could have, but did not. Like the priest, he passes by on the other side. He too failed to display the attributes of compassion. But the least likely candidate does. Here comes Mr. Samaritan.

Samaritans were considered a low class of people by the Jews since they intermarried with non-Jews and did not revere all of the commandments of the Mosaic Law. Jews detested Samaritans and would have nothing to do with Samaritans, accept for a Jew by the name of Jesus. Throughout His ministry Jesus engaged Himself with Samaritans. Jesus welcomed Samaritans into His fold. This interaction infuriated the Pharisees, Sadducees and the scribes. Nevertheless, Jesus embraced Samaritans and uses one to pitch the moral of His parable.

In the parable we do not know if the injured man was a Jew or Gentile, but we do know it made no difference to the Samaritan. He did not consider race or religion, but saw a person in need. Unlike the priest or Levite, he involves himself. We are told, *"When he saw him, he had compassion"* (v. 33). *Compassion* is "a feeling of deep sympathy and sorrow for another who is stricken by misfortune, accompanied by a strong desire to alleviate the suffering." The text says, *"He went to him and bandaged his wounds, pouring on oil and wine"* (v. 34). The *wine* was a disinfectant, and the *oil* served as ointment to sooth the pain. He then puts *"him on his own animal,"* (v.34), takes him to an inn and looks after him. He did not see him and neglect him. He did not see him and ignore him. He intervenes. He steps in. He intercedes at his own expense. This is what God did for us. This is what God continues to do. The Bible says, *"For God so loved the world, that He gave His only Begotten Son"* (John 3:16). Love sacrifices. Love mediates. Love facilitates. Love does not discriminate. Love does not see color. Love does not see race. Love does not see gender. Love does not limit itself. The question is: "Who is my neighbor?" A better question is: "Whom do we love?" To love God is to love others, without which, we lie about loving God (see 1 John 4).

The *Samaritan* saw his neighbor as the person in need. It did not matter the location. It did not matter the danger. He saw need and involved himself. He saw need and gave of himself. He gave up his animal. He gave up his wine. He gave up his oil. He gave up his money. Giving up is the Kingdom way. Helping out is Christ-like. The question is: "Who is my neighbor?" If one is hungry, this is our neighbor. If one is thirsty, this is our neighbor. If one is hurt, this is our neighbor. If beaten down, this is our neighbor. It is not enough to know the Law, but love is lifestyle. Love is conduct. It visits. It clothes. It feeds. It ministers. Love says, "If I can help somebody," "If I can cheer somebody," "If I can mend somebody," then my living is not in vain. The question is: "Who is my neighbor?"

Our neighbor is the cancer victim and the child who has been molested. It is the orphaned, and the widowed, and the sick, and senior citizen. It is anyone who has been rejected, or ostracized, or persecuted, or mistreated. It is the locked up and locked out. It is the suicidal and disheartened. It is the poor, the overlooked, the underpaid, and victimized. It is Trayvon Martin. It is Michael Brown. It is Hadiya Pendleton, and all the others. It is New Orleans. It is Africa. It is Haiti. It is Ferguson, MO. Where there is need, there is a neighbor. Where there is injustice, there is a neighbor. Dr. Martin Luther King, Jr. said, "Injustice anywhere threatens justice everywhere" (*Letter from a Birmingham Jail*). Who is my neighbor?

Jesus teaches us to apply the love principle wherever love is needed. If it is needed, do it. If it is needed, express it. If it is needed, live it. If it is needed, be it. Be a neighbor. Be a friend. Be a comfort. Make a difference. Be a Good Samaritan. Show mercy. Be a Good Samaritan. Demonstrate grace. Be a Good Samaritan—exhibit Christ. Start living what the Word teaches. Replicate the Samaritan model. Do it every day. Be compassionate. Be caring. Be considerate. Be concerned. Our neighbor is *need*. If we can help out, we should. If we have it, we should share it. Jesus says, *"Go and do likewise"* (v. 37). Help the helpless and offer hope. Help the homeless and offer hope. Help the hurting and offer hope. Stop along the way. Spread love's message that Jesus taught. BE A GOOD SAMARITAN!

CHAPTER 7

RICH MAN, POOR MAN
Parable of the Rich Man and the Beggar

Luke 16:19-31

[19]"There was a certain rich man who was clothed in purple and fine linen and fared sumptuously every day. [20] But there was a certain beggar named Lazarus, full of sores, who was laid at his gate, [21] desiring to be fed with the crumbs which fell from the rich man's table. Moreover the dogs came and licked his sores. [22] So it was that the beggar died, and was carried by the angels to Abraham's bosom. The rich man also died and was buried. [23] And being in torments in Hades, he lifted up his eyes and saw Abraham afar off and Lazarus in his bosom. [24]"Then he cried and said, 'Father Abraham, have mercy on me, and send Lazarus that he may dip the tip of his finger in water and cool my tongue; for I am tormented in this flame.'[25] But Abraham said, 'Son, remember that in your lifetime you received your good things, and likewise Lazarus evil things; but now he is comforted and you are tormented. [26] And besides all this, between us and you there is a great gulf

fixed, so that those who want to pass from here to you cannot, nor can those from there pass to us.' [27] "Then he said, 'I beg you therefore, father, that you would send him to my father's house, [28] for I have five brothers, that he may testify to them, lest they also come to this place of torment.' [29] Abraham said to him, 'They have Moses and the prophets; let them hear them.' [30] And he said, 'No, father Abraham; but if one goes to them from the dead, they will repent.' [31] But he said to him, 'If they do not hear Moses and the prophets, neither will they be persuaded though one rise from the dead.'"

⁘⁘⁘

In Chapter Six we explored the question of *who is my neighbor* and deduced it to be, based upon the illustrative parable presented to us by Jesus, anyone who is in need. Last chapter's parable, the *Parable of the Good Samaritan*, addressed the duty of human to human. It underscored our responsibility to do what we can to exemplify the love principle of *loving our neighbor as we love ourselves* (see Leviticus 19:18). Before us is another parable of Jesus that dramatizes this divine expectation of human obligation. It also visualizes the eternal ramification of negligence. It is called *The Parable of the Rich Man and the Beggar*. It is the story of two men, one rich, one poor, that tells of the relationship in life, as well as in death, between an unnamed rich man and a poor diseased beggar by the name of 'Lazarus.' The *Lazarus* of this parable is not to be confused with the *Lazarus*, who is the brother of Mary and Martha, whom Jesus raised from the dead. They are two distinct characters—one may be strictly fictitious, while the other one is real. However, both may be the names of actual persons.

Some theologians view the story of the *Rich Man and Lazarus* as an actual event that Jesus shares with His followers to communicate, yet again, a message to the Pharisees. These religious leaders once again derided Jesus in an attempt to sabotage His ministry and slander His character. Supporters of this interpretation point to a key detail in the parable, which is the use of a personal name that is not existent in any other parable of Jesus. By contrast, in all of His other parables, Jesus refers to a central character by a description and not a name, such as "a certain man," and so forth. In this parable, at least one of the central characters is given a name, and not just any name, but the name of *Lazarus*.

The name *Lazarus* has relevance or significance, for even the name conveys a message. The name means "God is my help," and we see in the parable that despite a life of suffering and rejection, in the end, Lazarus found comfort in the bosom of Abraham. In this I say, *never lose hope*. Psalm 46:1 declares, *"God is our refuge and strength, a very present help in trouble."* Always remember, no matter what we face in life, in God there is consolation and contentment. Though people may shun and shirk you, God will not. This is why David says, *"I will lift up mine eyes unto the hills, from whence cometh my help; my help cometh from the LORD, which made Heaven and earth"* (Psalm 121:1-2).

In the *Parable of the Rich Man and Lazarus*, Jesus draws on images from Jewish folklore. His listeners would have realized such, as Jesus describes a fixed gulf between the eternal placement of the rich man and that of Lazarus. Jesus does so in order to show the gulf or gap between arrogant people and individuals who become a part of the Kingdom of God. As we speak of Heaven, some people you expect to be there will not, and some you do not will. *Folklore* is "a popular myth, belief, custom, or story that is passed through generations by word of mouth, often unsupported, but widely circulated." In the story of the *Rich Man and Lazarus*, Jesus paints a riveting scene of contrasts. Here depicted are: riches and poverty, Heaven and Hell, compassion and apathy, inclusion and exclusion. We also see an abrupt noteworthy reversal of fortune. In life, we see rich man as rich man and poor man as poor man. In death, rich man becomes cursed man and poor man becomes blessed man. This is because in God's economy, those who hold on possessively to what they have lose it all in the end, while those who share gain even more. Jesus says, *"What shall it profit a man, if he gain the whole world, and lose his own soul"* (Mark 8:36)? Proverbs 11:25 asserts, *"A generous person will prosper [and] whoever refreshes others will be refreshed"* (NIV). In the parable, during his life the rich man treated the beggar (Lazarus) with contempt and indifference, but at the conclusion of life, he found his own fortunes inverted. In life, he lived in luxury and comfort, but in death, only anguish and torment. In death, he who ignored the plight of the beggar became a beggar himself. In other words, the generosity he negated to give was negated to him in the afterlife. His plea for relief did not matter. What was done was done.

Beyond the grave there is no grace. Beyond the grave there is no mercy. Beyond the grave there is no opportunity of forgiveness—beyond the grave, no second chance. It is somewhat hard to pull from this parable details about the afterlife, but one thing is sure—there is a place called *Heaven* and one called *Hell*. The text says "Hades" (v. 23), but "Hades" is synonymous with "Hell." *Hell* is reserved for those who selfishly spend their time on earth with no regard for others. This lifestyle and mindset contradicts the heart of God and mission of Jesus.

Hell is a real place for unbelievers. It is also for those who collaborate with the works of darkness. *Hell* was fashioned for Satan and the fallen angels, but according to Isaiah 5:14 it has enlarged itself beyond measure to include the wicked of this world. Once we die, we either will be carried away by the angels, as Lazarus was, or numbered among the eternal occupants of Hell, as was the rich man. Once we leave here our fate is sealed. Before we leave here there is choice. We have a choice, whether or not to care and share. We have a choice, whether or not to give and love. We have a choice, whether or not to be sympathetic or apathetic. We have a choice, whether or not to please God or self. There are so many lessons within this parable, but what is the central point of the parable? Remember, every parable has one. So what message does Jesus communicate? What is the symbolism of the parable? Who is this *rich man* and who is Lazarus? To answer these we must incorporate the context of the text.

Beginning at verse 14 it is written,

> Now the Pharisees, who were lovers of money, also heard all
> these things, and they derided Him. And He [Jesus] said to
> them, "you are those who justify yourselves before men, but
> God knows your hearts. For what is highly esteemed among
> men is an abomination in the sight of God.
>
> Luke 16:14-15

Clearly, the *rich man* represents the Pharisees and the Jewish nation as a whole. The Jews and their religious leaders had been blessed above measure with knowledge of God and His plan of salvation. They had received the adoption, the glory, the covenants, the Law, the service of God, as well as the divine promises of God (see Romans 9:4). They were of the seed of Abraham, and only Jews would pray to "Father Abraham." This is the case within the story of Luke 16:19-31.

Although they are not given a name, it is clear the Jews are represented by character. By contrast, *Lazarus* symbolizes all the people in spiritual poverty, in particular the Gentiles with whom the Israelites were to share their heritage. But instead of sharing, like many of us, they deprived others of the grace and blessings they had received from God. Going back to chapter 15, the religious leaders had a problem with Jesus' embrace of sinners and His invitation of salvation to sinners. In fact, it was this objection that propelled Jesus into a series of parables: the *Parable of the Lost Sheep*, the *Parable of the Lost Coin*, the *Parable of the Lost Son*, the *Parable of the Unjust Steward*, a brief lecture on the Law, the Prophets, and the Kingdom, and into our *Parable of the Rich Man, Poor Man*. In all of these Jesus seeks to promote the Kingdom agenda and what God expects of those who desire Him, which is the motive of all Jesus taught in parable and without parable.

In this chapter's parable, the rich man could not see beyond his material wealth and possessions. He not only had everything he needed but, like some of us, he selfishly spent all he had on himself. Like some of us, he was too enchanted with what he had to notice the needs of those around him. Like some of us, he lost sight of God, and like some of us, he became preoccupied with the accumulation and enjoyment of material things. In life, he served wealth rather than God. In death, he reaped the consequence of his failure to share his blessings with others.

In the text of Luke 16:19-31 we are told, *"there was a certain beggar named Lazarus, full of sores, who was laid at his gate, desiring to be fed with the crumbs which fell from the rich man's table"* (vv. 20-21). It goes on to say, *"Moreover the dogs came and licked his sores"* (v. 21). *Dogs* in the ancient world symbolized contempt or disapproval. Thus, being licked by dogs only added to Lazarus' misery and pain, and it increased his humiliation and degradation. Lazarus was not only poor, but he was sick, infectious, and beleaguered by dogs. He was laid at the gate, and in this we can deduce he could not walk. Being destitute and helpless, without food or assistance, Lazarus soon died, and *"the rich man also died and was buried"* (v. 22). No matter the status here, we all die. The Bible teaches us that in death, *"the rich and the poor meet together"* (Proverbs 22:2). In this world the rich and poor may live in different worlds and travel different paths, but God is the Maker of us all. Death has no favorites. Lazarus died, and so did the rich man. But Lazarus *"was carried by the angels to Abraham's bosom"* (v. 22). The rich man was tormented in Hell (v. 23). *"He lifted up his eyes and saw Abraham afar off, and Lazarus in his bosom"* (v. 23) and cried out for mercy. But *mercy* begets *mercy*. We reap what we sow (see Galatians 6:9). In life he showed 'no mercy.' In death he acquired the same. In life he could have provided shelter, food, and medical attention, but did nothing. This is the point of the parable. In life we can choose to do something or nothing. This is our prerogative. But Jesus seeks to teach us that earthly choices have eternal consequences. In other words, beyond this life what we do or fail to do in life will follow us past the grave. The Bible says, *"Blessed are the dead which die in the Lord from henceforth: Yea, saith the Spirit, that they may rest from their labors; and their works do follow them"* (Revelation 14:13). It also says, *"After death comes judgment"* (Hebrews 9:27). In judgment there is an analysis of life.

The lesson is: help somebody. The lesson is: feed somebody. The lesson is: serve somebody. The lesson is: we should do what we can while we can. It is getting late in the evening. There is a Lazarus at our gate. There is a Lazarus in trouble. There is a Lazarus in need. There is a Lazarus who is hungry. There is a Lazarus who is hurt. There is a Lazarus who is incapacitated. There is a Lazarus who is devastated. There is a Lazarus who is downtrodden. There is a Lazarus who is victimized. Every hospital has a Lazarus. Every prison has a Lazarus. Every nursing home has a Lazarus. Every neighborhood has a Lazarus. God is calling us to the gate to uplift Lazarus—to feed Lazarus—to nurture Lazarus—to protect Lazarus—to invite a Lazarus in. At the gate we must do something. At the gate we must give something. We must not forget that in the end God will flip the script. 'Nothing from nothing leaves nothing.'

Jesus says, *"The first shall be last and the last shall be first"* (Matthew 19:30). It is the end result that counts. It is the end result that matters. The nursery rhyme says, "Rich man, poor man, beggar man, thief, doctor, lawyer, Indian chief" (Tinker Tailor). It does not matter who we are. We have a duty to one another. We have a duty to love each other. We have a duty to help each other. We have a duty to provide comfort. We have a duty to ease burdens. God desires us to be like Him. God cares and gives. He intercedes and alleviates. This is what God did for us when He gave His Son to Calvary's cross. In the last chapter I was looking for a Good Samaritan. The search is still on. The harvest is still ripe. The search is still on. The need is still great. The search is still on. What can you render? What can you give? What will you do? What will you share? LAZARUS NEEDS OUR HELP!

Chapter 8

What Type Of Ground Are You?

Parable of the Sower and the Seed

Matthew 13:1-9; 18-23

¹On the same day Jesus went out of the house and sat by the sea. ² And great multitudes were gathered together to Him, so that He got into a boat and sat; and the whole multitude stood on the shore. ³ Then He spoke many things to them in parables, saying: "Behold, a sower went out to sow. ⁴ And as he sowed, some seed fell by the wayside; and the birds came and devoured them. ⁵ Some fell on stony places, where they did not have much earth; and they immediately sprang up because they had no depth of earth. ⁶ But when the sun was up they were scorched, and because they had no root they withered away. ⁷ And some fell among thorns, and the thorns sprang up and choked them. ⁸ But others fell on good ground and yielded a crop: some a hundredfold, some sixty, some thirty. ⁹ He who has ears to hear, let him hear!"

vv. 18b-23

"...Therefore hear the parable of the sower: [19] when anyone hears the Word of the Kingdom, and does not understand it, then the wicked one comes and snatches away what was sown in his heart. This is he who received seed by the wayside. [20] But he who received the seed on stony places, this is he who hears the Word and immediately receives it with joy; [21] yet he has no root in himself, but endures only for a while. For when tribulation or persecution arises because of the Word, immediately he stumbles. [22] Now he who received seed among the thorns is he, who hears the Word, and the cares of this world and the deceitfulness of riches choke the Word, and he becomes unfruitful. [23] But he who received seed on the good ground is he who hears the Word and understands it, who indeed bears fruit and produces: some a hundredfold, some sixty, some thirty."

As we look around the church and world, we quickly discover that few professing Christians are actually living productive spiritual lives. Everywhere we turn we find people who have been exposed to the teachings of Scripture. Despite this, many of the lives of the same people have not been changed. Despite this, the same people make little or no impact for the Kingdom of God. But then there are those who do. Jesus tells a parable that illustrates why some people are unfruitful, while others are. In the parable He compares lives and hearts to various types of ground on which seed is sown. From the parable we learn that the internal conditions must be right in order for God's Word to produce a harvest through us. We learn that there are things in the world that compete with the Word. We learn that, if we allow them, these things will dissipate the Word that has been sown in our hearts.

This parable is one of the most familiar of all of Jesus' parables. It is aptly called *the Parable of the Sower*. It is recorded in three of the four Gospel accounts—Matthew 13, Mark 4, and Luke 8. These three books are referred to as the "Synoptic Gospels." In the Greek language *synoptic* means, "seeing or viewing together." With this definition in mind, Matthew, Mark, and Luke are labeled such because the three chronicle many of the same events in the life and ministry of Jesus. These events are often recorded in similar sequence and phraseology.

The Parable of the Sower, sometimes referred to as The Parable of the Soils, introduces a series of seven parables that are documented in the 13th chapter of Matthew. The other six are: *The Parable of the Wheat and the Tares, The Parable of the Mustard Seed, The Parable of the Leaven, The Parable of the Hidden Treasure, The Parable of the Pearl of Great Price*, and *The Parable of the Dragnet*. All seven are communicated to a multitude of people as Jesus is sitting in a boat on the Sea of Galilee. Remember from previous chapters that a 'parable' is a story which utilizes familiar things in order to impart a spiritual truth or principle. Jesus begins the *Parable of the Sower* by saying, *"Behold, a sower went out to sow"* (v. 3). I recently visited

Israel and observed the magnitude of agriculture throughout the land. Farming, without question, is a subject matter Jesus' listeners were well acquainted with. In fact, although more than half of the land area is desert, still Israel produces 95 percent of its own food requirements. Thus, when Jesus says, *"a sower went out to sow,"* those who heard Him understood Jesus' metaphorical illustration.

Many times when the *Parable of the Sower* is expounded, the emphasis is on the representation of the *sower* and the *seed*. However, I want to underscore the type of ground the seed falls on. In the parable, the *sower* and the *seed* remains the same, but the ground of distribution varies. It is the variance of the ground that affects the penetration and effectiveness of the seed. The seed does not change. It remains the same, but the ground changes. By interpretation, the *seed* signifies the *"Word of the Kingdom"* (v. 19). The different grounds depict the different responses people have to the communication of the *Word of the Kingdom*. The different responses are based upon: attentiveness, environment, sincerity of interest, priority, preeminence, and application, or the lack thereof. In the *Parable of the Sower* there are four different terrains of broadcast. The text informs us that some seed fell by the wayside, some on stony places, some among thorns, and some on good ground. Thanks to the inquisitiveness of His disciples we have the interpretation of all four. The communication of the parable spans verses three through eight. The explanation of the parable is contained within verses eighteen through twenty-three. In verse nineteen this is what Jesus says, *"When anyone hears the Word of the Kingdom, and does not understand it, then the wicked one comes and snatches away what was sown in his heart. This is he who received seed by the wayside."* The birds that devour in verse four are deciphered as "the wicked one" in verse nineteen. In Mark's account this *wicked one* is "Satan" (4:15), and in Luke's account it says "the devil" (8:12). He comes *"immediately and takes away the Word that was sown in their hearts"* (Mark 4:15). In Luke it is written, *"Lest they should believe and be saved"* (8:12). In John 10:10 Jesus did say he is *"a thief, who comes to steal, kill, and to destroy."*

The *wayside* ground represents those who hear with the ear but do not receive with the heart. In order for the Word to be fruitful, the heart must be receptive. The heart cannot be calloused—it must be opened to what the Spirit has to say. The Word of God is not hard to understand, but when the heart is not opened to understanding, there can be no understanding. In this, Jesus is referring to people whose hearts are so hard that the truth of His Word cannot penetrate their lives. Just as seed cannot grow unless it penetrates the ground, so God's Word cannot grow unless it penetrates the heart. The heart that is primed for God's Word becomes a student of God's Word. It goes to Sunday School. It goes to Bible Study. It avails itself to teaching and interpretation. This is the heart that is faithful, available, and teachable. When seed falls by the wayside, it is susceptible to Satan.

In verse twenty Jesus explains the seed on *stony* places:

This is he who hears the Word and immediately receives it with joy; yet he has no root in himself, but endures only for a while, for when tribulation or persecution arises because of the Word, immediately he stumbles.

vv. 20-21

On stony surfaces, the reason the seed cannot survive is because the stones interfere with rootage. Without rootage, all things eventually wither away. Every plant must have root. Every tree must have root. Every flower must have root. Every Christian must have root. A dance and a song are not sufficient. We need the Word of God. We need a prayer life. We need constant fellowship with the saints. People who church hop have no root. People who make cameo appearances have no root. People who spectate instead of participate have no root. People who shout but do not serve have no root. Jesus says, *"These immediately receive the Word with gladness"* (v. 20), but when trouble comes because of the Word, the same fall away. The Word has no root and so the people stumble. If you are going to make it through the storms of life, then your soul must be anchored in the Word of God. The Bible says, *"A double-minded man is unstable in all his ways"* (James 1:8).

The seed among *thorns* is the Word of God among people. These embrace the Word of God, but also the ways of the world. These mix it up. They are lukewarm saints who straddle the fence, serve two masters, travel two roads, drink two different wines, and call upon different gods. Jesus says, *"These hear the Word, and the cares of this world and the deceitfulness of riches choke the Word, and he becomes unfruitful"* (v. 22). The message is: we cannot mix it up. We must make up our mind to either live for God or not. Matthew 6:33 declares, *"But seek first the Kingdom of God and His righteousness, and all these things shall be added to you."* Do not allow worldliness to choke the Word. Do not drain your spiritual energy with worldly passions. Pull up the weeds. Weeds extinguish life. Let the Word of God find in you good ground.

Good ground relates to people who hear the Word of God, understand the Word of God, and apply the Word of God. These people produce fruit for the Kingdom. Jesus says, *"some a hundredfold, some sixty and some thirty"* (v. 8). They hear the Word of God. They believe the Word of God. They love the Word of God. They share the Word of God. They preach it and practice it. What are you? What type of ground are you? Is your heart receptive to the Word of God? Does the Word of God take root in your heart? Are you a fair-weathered Christian or faithful Christian? Is your life good ground? Are you bearing any fruit? Is God glorified through your life? Jesus says, *"Herein is My Father glorified, that ye bear much fruit; so shall ye be My disciples"* (John 15:8). WHAT TYPE OF GROUND ARE YOU?

Chapter 9

Don't Be A Fool

Parable of the Rich Fool

Luke 12:13-21

[13] Then one from the crowd said to Him, "Teacher, tell my brother to divide the inheritance with me." [14] But He said to him, "Man, who made Me a judge or an arbitrator over you?" [15] And He said to them, "Take heed and beware of covetousness, for one's life does not consist in the abundance of the things he possesses." [16] Then He spoke a parable to them, saying: "The ground of a certain rich man yielded plentifully. [17] And he thought within himself, saying, 'What shall I do, since I have no room to store my crops?' [18] So he said, 'I will do this: I will pull down my barns and build greater, and there I will store all my crops and my goods. [19] And I will say to my soul, "Soul, you have many goods laid up for many years; take your ease; eat, drink, and be merry."' [20] But God said to him, 'Fool! This night your soul will be required of you; then whose will those things be which you have provided?' [21] "So is he who lays up treasure for himself, and is not rich toward God."

We turn again to another story that Jesus tells in response to something asked of Him. As He is doing what He routinely did, sharing lessons about the Kingdom of God, Jesus is abruptly interrupted by a man who is dissatisfied over what he considers to be an unfair division of his father's inheritance between himself and his brother. He approaches Jesus, imploring Jesus to meditate the matter, no doubt, in his favor. Apparently, he is the younger of the two brothers. According to Jewish law, the eldest brother executes the estate and, as the inheritor of the birthright, the eldest is the one who receives the largest portion of the father's inheritance. The eldest would receive, at least, a double portion of the inheritance. The younger would get less. In this particular case, the younger brother was not content with what was allocated to him in the distribution of his father's inheritance. So he seeks out Jesus for intervention. He literally, if you notice verse thirteen, demands of Jesus that He tell his brother to divide the inheritance with him. He does not ask Jesus, but demands. He says to Jesus, *"Teacher, tell my brother to divide the inheritance with me"* (v. 13). However, Jesus does not answer as expected to do, nor does He allow Himself to be sidetracked from His mission. His mission was to seek and to save the lost, not to arbitrate sibling disputes. Jesus says, *"Man, who made me a judge or an arbitrator over you"* (v. 14)? Instead of making a legal judgment, Jesus makes a moral one. Jesus knew that this family feud over inheritance was only a symptom of a greater problem, which was *greed*. In other words, the complaint to Jesus only camouflaged a covetous spirit, and with such an appetite of greed, no amount of settlement would satisfy. In fact, greed is never satisfied, which helps casinos stay in the business of taking our money. Casinos invest in our greed with free beverages and discounted meals, and even with money to get us started. What happens 'if' or 'when' we win? Most often, we keep playing because greed pushes us to win even more. Most often, we lose what we have won, and even more.

Greed or *covetousness* is a sin that always seeks more. It craves more. It desires more. It even steals and kills for more when it cannot have what it wants (see James 4:2). The Tenth Commandment of Exodus 20 forbids it, and all of Scripture speaks against it. Colossians 3:5 says, *"Covetousness is idolatry,"* and in Mark 7:22 Jesus lists it among other immoralities that defiles us. *Greed or covetousness* is dangerous because it is marked by an excessive yearning for wealth or possessions, or for that which belongs to someone else—someone else's wife—someone else's husband—someone else's property—someone else's life. *Covetousness* instigates murder, adultery, thievery, lying, cheating, corruption, exploitation, and so much more. In fact, *covetousness* instigates all other sins. Name the sin. We do it because self seeks to gratify itself. The person with greed in their heart is the person who finds happiness and comfort in material things and flesh, and not God. Do not be a fool! The things of this world will never placate (soothe) the longings of the soul. There is a place within us only God can pacify. There is a place within us only reserved for a relationship with God. Money cannot fulfill it. Sex cannot fulfill it. Drugs cannot fulfill it. Nothing or no one can. We were created for communion with our Creator.

In Luke 12:13-21, Jesus uses the disruption as a teachable moment. He says, *"Take heed and beware of covetousness, for one's life does not consist in the abundance of the things he possesses"* (v. 15). From this statement Jesus initiates a parable to illustrate and communicate, by way of story, that life is so much more than acquiring wealth. His story is not a narrative against wealth, but a parable about priorities. In fact, in the parable Jesus teaches us that possessions have a way of distracting us from true wealth. True wealth is not the accumulation of stuff or accretion of money, but how we view and what we do with what we have. True wealth entails the acknowledgment of God as Giver of all things. True wealth's message is: "God owns all, we own nothing." It is also: "We have because God gives." True wealth recognizes that we are not blessed to hoard, but to use our wealth to bless others, as well as to further the work of the Kingdom here on earth. This is the premise of "stewardship." *Stewardship* is based on the realization that everything belongs to God. A 'steward' uses the resources supplied by God to accomplish the purpose(s) of God. Psalm 62:10 declares, *"If riches increase, do not set your heart on them."* In other words, we are not to allow possessions to possess us. Instead, we are to use possessions to the glory of God. Instead, we are to count our blessings, but not embrace our blessings with no regard for the needs of anyone else. We cannot ignore the poor, or the homeless, or others who are destitute when we can do something to help.

The parable of Luke 12:13-21 is known as *The Parable of the Rich Fool*. It is labeled such because Jesus gives a hypothetical account about a rich farmer. This rich farmer has a field that yields a great crop, and the first thing he considers to do is to tear down his existing barns and build larger ones in order to keep his harvest to himself. Like too many of us, he does not consider anyone else but himself. His plan was early retirement. His plan was to take it easy. His plan was to eat and drink. His plan was to live the good life. He does not consider, what is unsaid in the parable, God's grace in causing the land to produce in abundance. There is no mention that he worked hard, only that *"the ground of a certain rich man yielded plentifully"* (v. 16). We must understand that in all things God gives the increase. Nothing grows without God. Nothing materializes without God. Without God we are like ships without a sail. The lesson is: we should never overlook what God does for us. The lesson is: we should never take for granted what God does for us, nor should we omit Him in the credits. The rich farmer considers no one but himself. He does not think about how he could help someone else. Like so many of us, he was only interested in managing his increase and storing up his growing prosperity.

The parable is referred to as *The Parable of the Rich Fool* because God calls him a *fool*. It is recorded in verse twenty. A "fool" in biblical language is not a description of mental ability, but spiritual discernment. After the farmer says, *"Soul, you have many goods laid up for many years; take your ease; eat, drink, and be merry"* (v. 19), God then pronounces him a fool. *"Fool! This night your soul will be required of you; then whose will those things be which you have provided"* (v. 20)? Why does God call him a *fool*? God calls him a fool because he only lives for himself. He thinks he can secure his life with possessions. This is foolish. It is foolish to live life selfishly. It is foolish to put one's trust in possessions. Possessions are here today and can be gone today. He is not called a fool because he is wealthy and saves for the future, but because he flatters himself by thinking he had a long lease on life to enjoy what he had. According to Jesus, we are likewise fools if we think and live as he (see verse 21). The Book of James teaches us that such an attitude is foolish. It teaches us that life is but a vapor. In other words, we only appear for a little time and soon vanish away (see James 4:13- 16). In addition to James, life teaches us that tomorrow is not promised to any of us. In fact, today's sunset is not guaranteed. I was taught we should say, *"If the Lord wills"* (James 4:16). Do not be a fool!

We are fools if we fail to acknowledge God for the things He does. We are fools if we make plans, but leave God out. We are fools if we think there is no God. Psalm 14:1 reads, *"The fool says in his heart, 'there is no God.'"* It is not the verbalization of "there is no God" that makes one a fool, but it is when we live life as if God does not exist. Such is a fool! Fools leave God out. Fools do not recognize any obligation to God. Fools get up in the morning and say nothing to God. Fools eat food and say nothing to God. Fools dress themselves and say nothing to God. Fools go to church and give nothing to God. I say, "That is a fool!" It is God who wakes us up in the morning. It is God who provides food for our tables. It is God who places a roof over our head. It is God who supplies us with money. Do not be a fool! We are fools when we only live for the moment. We are fools when we store our wealth in the wrong place. Jesus says,

> Do not lay up for yourselves treasures on earth, where moth and rust destroy and where thieves break in and steal, but lay up for yourselves treasures in Heaven, where neither moth nor rust destroys and where thieves do not break in and steal.
>
> Matthew 6:19-20

I stated earlier that *true wealth* acknowledges God as Giver—Giver of all things—Giver of whatever we have. True wealth utilizes wealth to fund the work of God here on earth. Proverbs 21:26 declare, *"Some people are always greedy for more, but the godly love to give"* (NLT)! Do not be a fool! Do not live life for yourself. Do not think that tomorrow is guaranteed. What we possess does not assure us of tomorrow. Plans do not assure us of tomorrow. Plans do not always include us. Things, many times, outlive us. What we have today will be someone else's tomorrow. What happens when we die? All that we have is left behind. Someone else will wear our clothes. Someone else will drive our car. Someone else will own our home. Someone else will sleep in our bed. Our stuff becomes someone else's stuff. We cannot take it with us. We must leave it all behind. We must leave the money behind. We must leave the jewelry behind. We must leave the shoes behind. All that we have will be left behind. The grave has only room enough for us. *"We brought nothing into this world, and it is certain we can carry nothing out"* (1 Timothy 6:7). Do not be a fool! When you have been blessed, pass it on. With what you have, honor God.

We honor God when we share. We honor God when we give. We honor God when we help. We honor God when we consider someone else—when we visit the sick—when we feed the hungry—when we clothe the naked—when we do our part to keep them warm. Do not be a fool! Riches cannot insulate from hardship, sickness, disease, or death. Things cannot buy happiness or provide peace of mind. It is written,

> Command those who are rich in this present world not to be arrogant nor to put their hope in wealth, which is so uncertain, but to put their hope in God, who richly provides us with everything for our enjoyment; command them to do good, to be rich in good deeds, and to be generous and willing to share.
>
> 1 Timothy 6:17-18, NIV

Wealth is uncertain, but God is sure. Riches fail, but God is faithful. Wealth is temporary. God is eternal. If we honor Him with what we possess, God gives us even more. Do not be a fool! Do not be a penny-pincher! Do not be a tightwad! Open your hand and share. Open your hand and care. Open your hand and give. Open your hand and bring glory to God. God who gives can take away (see Job 1:21). So do not be a fool! God is Sovereign. God is in charge. Our life is in His Hands. Proverbs says, *"He who trusts in his riches will fall, but the righteous will flourish like foliage"* (11:28). DO NOT BE A FOOL!

Chapter 10

The Paradox of Humility

Parable of Taking the Lowest Place

Luke 14:1-11

[1] Now it happened, as He went into the house of one of the rulers of the Pharisees to eat bread on the Sabbath, that they watched Him closely. [2] And behold, there was a certain man before Him who had dropsy. [3] And Jesus, answering, spoke to the lawyers and Pharisees, saying, "Is it lawful to heal on the Sabbath?" [4] But they kept silent. And He took him and healed him, and let him go. [5] Then He answered them, saying, "Which of you, having a donkey or an ox that has fallen into a pit, will not immediately pull him out on the Sabbath day?" [6] And they could not answer Him regarding these things. [7] So He told a parable to those who were invited, when He noted how they chose the best places, saying to them: [8] "When you are invited by anyone to a wedding feast, do not sit down in the best place, lest one more honorable than you be invited by him; [9] and he who invited you and him come and say to

you, 'Give place to this man,' and then you begin with shame to take the lowest place. [10] But when you are invited, go and sit down in the lowest place, so that when he who invited you comes he may say to you, 'Friend, go up higher.' Then you will have glory in the presence of those who sit at the table with you. [11] For whoever exalts himself will be humbled, and he who humbles himself will be exalted."

L et me begin by defining the term 'paradox.' A *paradox* is "a statement or proposition that seems self-contradictory or absurd but in reality expresses a possible truth." A *paradox* combines two opposite things or terminologies, such as "humility" and "arrogance," in order to teach a lesson that may not seem possible in theory, but in actuality is. For example: "the paradox of war is peace." Although *war* and *peace* are divergent by definition, the premise is accepted as correct. *Peace* is obtained through *war*. William Shakespeare once said, "I must be cruel only to be kind." This is a line from his play "Hamlet" interpreting his malice toward his mother as a way of saving her. An examination of Scripture reveals that the Bible is filled with paradoxical declarations designed to teach us God's Will. Many sound irrational, but are reliable divine principles written to impart wisdom, caution, inspiration, motivation, and education. We gain strength through weakness (see 2 Corinthians 12:10). We receive through giving (see Luke 6:38). We are free through servitude (see Romans 6:18). We live through dying (see John 12:24). The first shall be last (see Mark 10:31). The way up is down (see Luke 14:11), which is the theme of this chapter's lesson. Its focus is on 'humility.'

Humility is defined as "a modest or low view of one's own importance." It is "the quality or condition of being humble." The word 'humble' means "not proud." By *proud* it means, 'not caught up in oneself' or 'thinking oneself better than others.' The reality is: none of us are any better than the rest of us. We may have more education, money, or material things than others, but none of these qualifies us as better. The Bible encourages us to look at ourselves with "sober judgment" (see Romans 12:3, NIV). *Sober judgment* urges 'self-examination.' *Self-examination* invites us to study our own behaviors and motivations—to inspect the *man* or *woman* in the mirror. Honest *self-inspection* will reveal some apparent realities. We all have blemishes. We all have imperfections. We all have inadequacies. We all have limitations. Isaiah 64:6 says, *"We are all like an unclean thing, and all our righteousness are like filthy rags."* Lest we forget: *"All have sinned and fall short of the glory of God"* (Romans 3:23). *"There is none righteous, no, not one"* (Romans 3:10).

Humility keeps us grounded. Humility keeps us unpretentious. Humility gives us the understanding that we all 'come from' and 'shall return' to the same source. God told Adam, *"For dust you are, and to dust you shall return"* (Genesis 3:19). Since we are all descendants of Adam, it shall be for all of us: "ashes to ashes," "dust to dust," and "earth to earth" (Book of Common Prayer).

It does not matter our accomplishments. We all came from dirt. We shall all die. We shall all stand before God. We shall all be judged by God. The reality is: a humbled life pleases God. The reality is: a humbled life is rewarded by God. *Humility* is how Jesus lived His life. *Humility* is how God wants us to live ours. It is not self-hatred, but self-denial. "Humility is not thinking less of yourself, but thinking of yourself less" (C.S. Lewis). Thinking of ourselves less is the best way to foster humility. This may be difficult for some to do, but among the sins that God hates is "a proud look" (see Proverbs 6:17).

A *proud look* is the catalyst for all sins. It is conceited. It is big-headed. It is full of itself. It thinks of no one else but self. A *proud look* disparages others and separates itself from others. It contradicts what Scripture teaches. Scripture teaches,

> Let nothing be done through selfish ambition or conceit, but in lowliness of mind let each esteem others better than himself. Let each of you look out not only for his own interests, but also for the interests of others. Let this mind be in you which was also in Christ Jesus.
>
> Philippians 2:3-5

In the flesh Jesus humbled Himself. He made Himself of no reputation. He served. He ministered. He considered others. He gave Himself to the cross. For this reason it is written,

> God also has highly exalted Him and given Him the Name which is above every name, that at the Name of Jesus every

knee should bow, of those in Heaven, and of those on earth, and of those under the earth, and that every tongue should confess that Jesus Christ is Lord, to the glory of God the Father.

Philippians 2:9-11

There is an upside to the downside of humility. *Humility* is the point of Jesus' parable. It is called *The Parable of Taking the Lowest Place* and illustrates the value of humility. The setting is in the house of one of the rulers of the Pharisees. Jesus is invited to eat bread on the Sabbath. We are told that "they watched Him closely" (v. 1). But as they watched Jesus, Jesus was doing surveillance Himself. He took note of *"how they chose the best places"* (v. 7). The *best places* were the seats of honor nearest the host. These were the V.I.P. (Very Important Person) seats, designated for distinguished guests. As they watched Jesus, Jesus watched them. He observes their ambitious movements, which prompted a story about *taking the lowest place.* In the story Jesus says,

> When you are invited by anyone to a wedding feast, do not sit down in the best place, lest one more honorable than you be invited by him; and he who invited you and him come and say to you, 'Give place to this man,' and then you begin with shame to take the lowest place. But when you are invited, go and sit down in the lowest place, so that when he who invited you comes he may say to you, 'Friend, go up higher.' Then you will have glory in the presence of those who sit at the table with you. For whoever exalts himself will be humbled, and he who humbles himself will be exalted.

vv. 7-11

What is the moral to the story? With this story Jesus teaches that *humility* is better than *humiliation*. The lesson is, as I was taught—it is far better to be asked up than to be asked down. In fact, it can be embarrassing to be asked down. According to Jesus, *humility* can eliminate an awkward situation. It can prevent us from looking bad. It can also make us look good. This is the paradox of humility. There are two options of outcome: honor or dishonor, praise or reprimand, exaltation or degradation, distinction or disgrace. In fact, the Bible says *"When pride comes, then comes disgrace, but with humility comes wisdom"* (Proverbs 11:2, NIV). Jesus says, *"Sit down in the lowest place"* (v. 10). Do not be moved to the lowest place. Take the lowest place and be asked to a higher place. *Humility* is better than pride. *"Pride goes before destruction, and a haughty spirit before a fall"* (Proverbs 16:18). The writer of James says, *"Humble yourselves before the Lord, and He will lift you up"* (James 4:10, NIV). Let God lift you up. Do not try to be 'Mister Big Stuff.' The song says, "Mr. Big Stuff, who do you think you are" (*Mr. Big Stuff*, Jean Knight).

Do not fool yourself and do not be a fool. Fancy clothes do not make us. Big cars do not make us. Diamond rings do not make us. Dollar bills do not make us. We can have it, but should not flaunt it. *Humility* brings honor, beauty, and praise. Scripture says, *"God opposes the proud, but gives grace to the humble"* (James 4:6, ESV). The message is: "Do not embarrass YOU." *Humility* is the way. Take the low place. Let God take you higher. Stop tooting your own horn—"Let someone else praise you" (Proverbs 27:2, NIV). Think less of self. Think more of others. Think most of God. Jesus says, *"But seek ye first the Kingdom of God"* (Matthew 6:33). The humbled life is a giving life. It serves. It shares. It sacrifices. It denies self for the sake of others. It does not seek the limelight, fame, or fortune. It is meek. It is gentle. It is modest. It is compassionate. The message is: "humility." Take the back seat. Take the lowest seat. *"Let this mind be in you, which was also in Christ Jesus"* (Philippians 2:5). Humility is the lesson. Humility is the way. GOD EXALTS A HUMBLE LIFE!

CHAPTER 11

DON'T LOSE HEART, KEEP PRAYING

Parable of the Persistent Widow

Luke 18:1-8

[1]Then He spoke a parable to them that men always ought to pray and not lose heart, [2] saying: "There was in a certain city a judge who did not fear God nor regard man. [3] Now there was a widow in that city; and she came to him, saying 'Get justice for me from my adversary.' [4] And he would not for a while; but afterward he said within himself, 'Though I do not fear God nor regard man, [5] yet because this widow troubles me I will avenge her, lest by her continual coming she weary me.'" [6] Then the Lord said, "Hear what the unjust judge said. [7] And shall God not avenge His own elect who cry out day and night to Him, though He bears long with them? [8] I tell you that He will avenge them speedily. Nevertheless, when the Son of Man comes, will He really find faith on the earth?"

Prayer is a major theme throughout the Gospel of Luke, as well as throughout all of Scripture. In the Eleventh Chapter of Luke, after observing Jesus pray, His disciples asked Him, *"Lord, teach us to pray, as John also taught his disciples"* (Luke 11:1). From this request we are given Luke's version of "The Lord's Prayer," also recorded in Matthew 6:9-13. Luke 18:1-8 is an extension of Jesus' teaching on *prayer*. It could easily be read in conjunction with the context of Luke 11:1-13. Where Luke 18 begins, the context of Luke 11 leaves off. There Jesus shares an illustrative story about a 'friend at midnight' to emphasize the importance of persistence. He also gives a brief discourse on the benefits of asking, seeking, and knocking to express God's pleasure in giving to those who petition Him (see Luke 11:9-13).

In the story before us the theme of persistence continues. Here we learn more of the value of persistent prayer, as well as the need for prayer in our lives—whether we care to acknowledge it or not, *prayer* is beneficial. In fact, 'prayer' is as beneficial to our spiritual survival as 'air' is to our physical endurance. In the physical, without the ability to breathe we become weak and soon die. In the spiritual, without prayer we become weak and susceptible to Satan's attacks. It is true: MUCH PRAYER, MUCH POWER. LITTLE PRAYER, LITTLE POWER. NO PRAYER, NO POWER. Never underestimate the worth of prayer. *Prayer* is a sin killer, sick healer, power giver, victory gainer, and a blessing promoter. Keep on praying. *Prayer* empowers us. Through prayer we gain strength, comfort, stability, and tranquility. In the hymn, "What a Friend We Have in Jesus," it is written: "Oh, what peace we often forfeit, oh, what needless pains we bear, all because we do not carry everything to God in prayer" (*What a Friend We Have in Jesus*, Joseph Scriven). *Prayer* makes us effective in our Christian walk. It equips us for spiritual warfare. It keeps our selfishness in check. It brings us closer to God. How important is prayer? Without prayer, spiritually, we suffocate. The more we neglect to pray, the more we distance ourselves from the Source of our help, which is God. We are encouraged in Scripture to *"pray without ceasing"* (1 Thessalonians 5:17). It is ceaseless prayer that is the thesis of Luke 18:1-5. *Ceaseless* means 'continual.' *Ceaseless* means 'constant.' *Ceaseless* means 'persistent,' 'perpetual,' 'permanent,' 'long-lasting,' and 'unending.' This does not mean we pray every minute of every day, but that prayer should be habitually a part of every day.

In His introduction to the parable Jesus says, *"Men always ought to pray and not lose heart"* (Luke 18:1). To *lose heart* means we become discouraged and prone to give up. It means we lose our courage or confidence. It means we stop believing we can succeed. It means we abandon our efforts and quit. In connection with prayer, to *lose heart* means that we *lose faith*. When petitioning God we should never lose faith. It is faith within prayer that gains God's attention. It is not the eloquence of our words, the pitch of our voice, the repetitiveness of our expressions, or the longevity of our dialogue. It is FAITH! *Faith* beckons God. *Faith* arouses God. *Faith* honors God. In prayer, *faith* is essential. Without faith, we cannot please God (see Hebrews 11:6). We must believe in His existence (see Hebrews 11:6). We must believe in His ability (see

Hebrews 11:6). God *"is a rewarder of them that diligently seek Him"* (Hebrews 11:6). The term 'diligent' is synonymous with the term 'persistent.' *Persistence* is unrelentingly resolved to do something in spite of difficulty, obstacle, frustration, or opposition. In other words, no matter what situations or circumstances may look like, sound like, or feel like, *persistence* does not give up. *Persistence* does not lose faith. *Persistence* does not lose heart. It stays the course. This is the lesson Jesus teaches concerning prayer. No matter what, we should keep praying. Faith believes that God is able.

The parable of Luke 18 is appropriately called, *The Parable of the Persistent Widow.* In its storyline there is a judge who does not fear God or care about what people think. One day he is approached by a widow who appeals to him for justice. We are not privy to her predicament, only her appeal for resolution. In Biblical time women, especially widows, had few legal rights. The Old Testament story of Ruth provides some detail on this. Ruth, along with her mother-in-law Naomi (*nah-oh-mee*), returned to Bethlehem as widows with no legal right to claim land once belonging to their husbands. Fortunately for Ruth there was a Boaz (*bow-as*), who became her 'kinsman redeemer.' A *kinsman redeemer* is a male relative who had the privilege or responsibility to act on behalf of a relative who was in trouble, danger, or need (see Leviticus 25:47-55; 27:9-25). The widow of Luke 18 probably had no *kinsman redeemer,* so she makes her appeal to the judge. Though we are unaware of her dilemma, we do know that her appeal was ongoing. According to the words of the judge she continued to appear before him (see verse 5). She would not give up. She would not go away. She was persistent. And I believe she was persistent because she knew the judge had the ability to help out. She knew he had the authority. She knew he had the power. So she kept coming. The message to us is: *keep coming. Keep praying. Do not give up. Do not lose heart.* God has the ability. God has the authority. God has the power. Nothing is too hard for Him (see Jeremiah 32:27). Jesus says, *"What is impossible with man is possible with God"* (Luke 18:27, AMP).

In this parable of Jesus the widow had to deal with an unjust judge, but she was persistent. Before the judge she stood time and time again until her persistence paid off. And because of her persistence she gained a verdict in her favor. Jesus tells this parable to teach us that God is waiting to hear from us. The message is: *God will avenge His own who cry out to Him day and night* (see verses 7-8). The message is: *do not worry.* The message is: *do not quit.* The message is: *do not doubt.* The message is: *do not lose heart, but keep on praying. Keep asking. Keep seeking. Keep knocking. "Have faith in God"* (Mark 11:22). *Faith* moves mountains. *Faith* calms fears. *Faith* produces miracles. *Faith* brings what we need to pass. Jesus says, *"Therefore I say to you, whatever things you ask when you pray, believe that you receive them, and you will have them"* (Mark 11:24). In prayer we must have faith! We must believe God can do it! We must believe God is able! There is no promise He cannot keep. There is no prayer He cannot answer. There is no problem He cannot solve. There is no person He cannot save. God can do it! Ephesians 3:20

declares, "*Now unto Him that is able to do exceedingly abundantly above all that we ask or think, according to the power that works in us.*" The "power" is our faith. *Faith* awakens God. *Faith* promotes God. *Faith* pleases God. *Faith* activates the favor of God. Keep believing. Do not lose heart, but keep praying.

Keep pursuing God. Keep calling out to God. Keep trusting God. Never doubt what God can do. PUSH! Pray until something happens! PUSH! Pray until someone hears! PUSH! Do not let go! PUSH! Do not give up! PUSH! Do not quit! PUSH! Do not lose heart! Keep praying! God will fight your battles. Keep praying! God will see you through. Keep praying! God will give you strength. Keep praying! God can turn your situation around. Pray in the morning! Pray in the noonday hour! Pray in the evening! Pray at midnight! God can do it! God can handle it! God can fix it! *Prayer can* make it alright! *Prayer* is our 3-1-1. *Prayer* is our 4-1-1. *Prayer* is our 9-1-1. Use it—prayer helps. Use it—God made it possible. Use it—it is a privilege. Use it— prayer works! "Oh, what peace we often forfeit, oh, what needless pains we bear, all because we do not carry everything to God in prayer" (*What a Friend We Have in Jesus*, Joseph Scriven, 1855). DO NOT LOSE HEART, KEEP PRAYING!

CHAPTER 12
THE SPIRIT OF PRAYER
Parable of the Pharisee and the Tax-Collector
Luke 18:9-14

[9]Also He spoke this parable to some who trusted in themselves that they were righteous, and despised others: [10] "Two men went up to the temple to pray, one a Pharisee and the other a tax collector. [11] The Pharisee stood and prayed thus with himself, 'God, I thank You that I am not like other men—extortioners, unjust, adulterers, or even as this tax collector. [12] I fast twice a week; I give tithes of all that I possess.' [13] And the tax collector, standing afar off, would not so much as raise his eyes to Heaven, but beat his breast, saying, 'God, be merciful to me a sinner!' [14] I tell you, this man went down to his house justified rather than the other; for everyone who exalts himself will be humbled, and he who humbles himself will be exalted."

In our last chapter we examined the parable before this parable, the *Parable of the Persistent Widow* (see Luke 18:1-8).

Both that parable and the one of this chapter are spoken by Jesus to teach valuable lessons on prayer. The *Parable of the Persistent Widow* spotlights the benefits of being tenacious in our petitions to God. In this parable, known as *the Parable of the Pharisee and the Tax-Collector*, the emphasis is on the type of spirit we bring into our prayer closets. It gives us an example of the wrong spirit contrasted against the kind of spirit God desires us to have, not only in our approach to Him in prayer, but also in our walk among others within life. In examining the *Parable of the Pharisee and Tax-Collector*, one can readily detect some noteworthy distinctions between the prayer of the Pharisee and that of the tax-collector, as well as how the two individuals view themselves. As we eavesdrop by permission of Scripture, we hear in one prayer the words of *self-righteousness*, in the other, the language of *self-effacement*.

Self-effacement is defined as "not drawing attention to oneself." It is characterized by an attitude of modesty, humility, unpretentiousness, and sincerity. People who are self-effacing tend to shun personal attention, as well as personal praise, tribute, credit, and glory. These people exhibit the type of spirit Jesus encourages for all of His followers, especially in His discourse on charitable deeds, fasting, and prayer (see Matthew 6:1-18). Jesus teaches us that whatever we do should be done in secret, and God, who sees what is done and hears what is said in secret, rewards us openly (see Matthew 6:1-18).

Contrasting *self-effacement* is *self-righteousness*. A *self-righteous spirit* thinks it is better than others, more worthy than others, more superior to others, and has an unfoundedly arrogant view of self. With people who are self-righteous no one is right but them, no one is good but them, no one is capable but them, and no one can compare to them. They are sanctimonious, holier-than-thou, pious, and preachy individuals who demean and degrade others in order to boost the appraisal of self. We all know the type. Self-righteous people are judgmental, smug, condescending, snobby, snooty, snotty, supercilious, and superficial. In order to make themselves look good, they look down on others, as well as talk down to others. *Self-righteous* people find no fault in themselves, but much fault in others. If you listen to them you would think they have no sin, weakness, flaws, depravity of disposition, imperfections, failings, immoral tendencies, or wicked skeletons within their past. But that would be inconsistent with the Word of God. In the Word of God it is written: *"For all have sinned and fall short of the glory of God"* (Romans 3:23). *"There is none righteous, no, not one"* (Romans 3:10). It also says, *"If we say that we have no sin, we deceive ourselves, and the truth is not in us"* (1 John 1:8). *"All of us, like sheep, have strayed away. We have left God's paths to follow our own"* (Isaiah 53:6, NLT).

The truth is: we all struggle. The truth is: we are all prone to fail. The truth is: at times we all miss the mark. The truth is: every day we all need God. We need God's mercy. We need God's grace. We need God's forgiveness. We need God's patience. I do not know about you, but I will admit that I am not perfect, and before you whisper about me, my reality is yours—you are not perfect. None of us are any better than the rest of us. Eating caviar does not make us better. Flying first-class does not make us better. Living in gated communities does not make us better. Having lots of money does not make us better. Wearing designer clothes does not make us better. Like the Pharisee of the parable, too many think too highly of themselves. However, the truth is: we all come from dirt and shall all return to dirt. No matter the achievements within life, in the end the pronouncement will be the same: "ashes to ashes, dust to dust, and earth to earth" (Book of Common Prayer). Scripture declares, *The rich and the poor meet together: the LORD is the Maker of them all*" (Proverbs 22:2). In other words, no matter what separates us in life, in death we shall come together. In death the grave dimensions are the same—2 ½ feet wide by 8 feet long. None of us will escape. There is an expiration date for us all, and before God we shall all stand. Before God we are all unworthy without the advocacy of Christ. So why embellish ourselves in life? In life, like the Pharisee of the parable, we like to compare ourselves to others. In doing so, we never look toward someone better off than us, always someone worse. The term for this is 'Comparisonitis.' *Comparisonitis* is an infectious disease that causes us to compare ourselves to others. We do so to determine, at least in our own assessment—prominence, distinction, popularity, and celebrity. In society it is used in the formation of social groups and social orders, as well as in the segregation and discrimination of races, genders, lifestyles, and localities.

Weeks ago seventeen lives were lost in France and national

leaders came together in solidarity, which is good, as well we should. However, where is the solidarity for the thousands of lives lost in Africa and other countries of the world? In God's heart, all souls matter. God makes no distinction between race, residency, culture, custom, or sin. In God's heart every one matters—a prostitute, drug addict, alcoholic, adulterer, or tax-collector. You name the sin—God still loves the sinner. In fact, from God's standpoint sin is sin. In God's judgment of sin there are no categories of difference or allowance for any. We may not have done what others have done, but a *sinner* is a sinner. It matters not the transgression, indiscretion, delinquency, or violation. Lying is a sin. Gossiping is a sin. Envy is a sin, and the list goes on. We need to rid ourselves of *comparisonitis* within our homes, communities, churches, and prayers. For this reason Jesus tells this parable. The motivation is recorded in verse nine.

There were those around Jesus, most likely Pharisees, who *"trusted in themselves that they were righteous, and despised others"* (vs. 9). *Despise* means they deplored others, as well as dismissed others as worthless or insignificant. So Jesus tells a story because all souls matter. He says,

> Two men went up to the temple to pray, one a Pharisee and the other a tax collector. The Pharisee stood and prayed thus with himself, 'God, I thank You that I am not like other men—extortioners, unjust, adulterers, or even as this tax collector. I fast twice a week; I give tithes of all that I possess.'
>
> vv. 10-12

Blah, blah, blah! I do not drink. I do not smoke. I do not sleep around. I do not cuss. I do not get high. I do not do this. I do not do that. I have never done this. I have never done that. So goes the testimonies of the *goody two shoes* self-righteous. But God is not concerned about us telling Him what we do not do. God is not blind. Nothing is a secret to Him: *"The eyes of the LORD are in every place, keeping watch on the evil and the good"* (Proverbs 15:3). God knows every righteous act and sinful deed. Instead of exalting ourselves in prayer, God would rather hear 'confession.' Like David, God would have us to *declare our ways* (see Psalm 119:26). In other words, God would have us to admit our sins and own up to our iniquities.

A Scottish proverb says, *"Open confession is good for the soul"* (source unknown), and it is. *Confession* cleanses us. *Confession* unburdens us. *Confession* restores us. *Confession* awakens us to our own conditions. God knows our sins. In confession we acknowledge what God already knows. *Prayer* affords us the opportunity to come clean with God, which benefits us. It is written, *"If we confess our sins, He [God] is just to forgive us our sins and to cleanse us from all unrighteousness"* (1 John 1:9). Instead of coming clean the Pharisee bragged on himself. He also denigrated the tax-collector. The tax-collector, however, *"standing afar off, would not so much as raise his eyes to Heaven"* (v. 13). With a gesture of shame, he beat his chest and cried out for mercy. In prayer, he acknowledges his sinfulness and goes home justified (see verse 14). *Justified* means, he was declared righteous. In other words, his sins were forgiven. In other words, his fellowship was restored. God justifies those who humble themselves. God rejects those who exalt themselves. This is the moral of the parable.

There is a difference between modesty and conceit. *Modesty looks* to God. *Conceit* promotes self. *Modesty* concedes to God. *Conceit* applauds self. Jesus says, *"When you pray, do not be like the hypocrites"* (Matthew 6:5, NIV). In other words, do not pray to booster self. In other words, do not pray to draw attention to self. But when we pray we should go into our secret closet (room, place, space), and when the door is shut pray:

> Our Father, which art in heaven, hallowed be thy name, thy kingdom come, thy will be done in earth, as it is in heaven. Give us this day our daily bread. And forgive us our debts, as we forgive our debtors. And lead us not into temptation, but deliver us from evil: for thine is the kingdom, and the power, and the glory, forever Amen.
>
> vv. 9-13

This is the spirit of prayer. God wants us to come to Him, but come with a humbled mind, heart, tongue, and spirit. God wants us to say, "Lord, I'm sorry." "Lord, forgive me." "Lord, clean me up." "Lord, make me whole." "It is me, O Lord, standing in the need of prayer." *"Create in me a clean heart; O God; and renew a right spirit within me"* (Psalm 51:10). "Wash me." "Cleanse me." "Purge me." "Lord, make me better!" Again I say: "we all need God." We need His mercy. We need His grace. We need His forgiveness. We need His patience.

There will come a time when titles will not matter. There will come a time when fame will not matter. There will come a time when fortune will not matter. There will come a time when trophies will not matter. In that time what will matter is what we have done to please the Lord. Did we do His will? Did we bring Him glory? Did we share His story? Did we help somebody? Did we feed the hungry? Did we clothe the naked? Did we visit the sick? Did we cheer a dejected soul? The lesson is: we should stop bragging on ourselves and boast in God. Without God we can do nothing and would have nothing. It should always be: "To God be the glory for the things He has done" (Andre Crouch, *My Tribute*). He saves us. He delivers us. He redeems us. He gives us another chance. The spirit of prayer is the spirit of humility and gratitude. Do you have it? ARE YOU THE PHARISEE OR TAX-COLLECTOR?

Chapter 13
A Tale of Two Sons

Parable of the Two Sons

Matthew 21:23-32

23 Now when He came into the temple, the chief priests and the elders of the people confronted Him as He was teaching, and said, "By what authority are You doing these things? And who gave You this authority?" 24 But Jesus answered and said to them, "I also will ask you one thing, which if you tell Me, I likewise will tell you by what authority I do these things: 25 the baptism of John—where was it from? From Heaven or from men?" And they reasoned among themselves, saying, "If we say, 'From Heaven,' He will say to us, 'Why then did you not believe him?' 26 But if we say, 'From men,' we fear the multitude, for all count John as a prophet." 27 So they answered Jesus and said, "We do not know." And He said to them, "Neither will I tell you by what authority I do these things. 28 "But what

do you think? A man had two sons, and he came to the first and said, 'Son, go, work today in my vineyard.' [29] He answered and said, 'I will not,' but afterward he regretted it and went.[30] Then he came to the second and said likewise. And he answered and said, 'I go, sir,' but he did not go. [31] Which of the two did the will of his father?" They said to Him, "The first." Jesus said to them, "Assuredly, I say to you that tax collectors and harlots enter the Kingdom of God before you. [32] For John came to you in the way of righteousness, and you did not believe him; but tax collectors and harlots believed him; and when you saw it, you did not afterward relent and believe him.

A 'tale' is a story. In Matthew 21:23-32 is a story by Jesus intended to serve as a mirror. Jesus wanted those who confronted Him to see themselves as they truly were—defiant, rebellious, disobedient, and unfruitful men in need of repentance. In fact, this is the aim of God's Word for us. The objective of God's Word is to get us to look at ourselves, make adjustments where necessary, and reflect the image of Jesus Christ in our lives, who is the express image of God the Father (see Romans 8:29; Hebrews 1:3). In John 14:9 Jesus tells an inquisitive Philip, *"Anyone who has seen Me has seen the Father"* (NIV).

The story of this chapter is called *The Parable of the Two Sons*. It is the by-product of yet another antagonist inquiry by certain leaders of the religious community. Oftentimes the Pharisees, Sadducees, and scribes opposed Jesus, this time it is the *chief priests* and the *elders*. They approach Jesus with an agenda to cripple His ministry and disintegrate His popularity. The *chief priests* were members of the high priestly families, or individuals who acted with the authority of the high priest. This faction of the religious community was in charge of temple worship. They also were regarded as the leading spokespersons of the Jewish people. The *elders* were community leaders and judges. They were an assembly of older men that were often members of an official governing council, such as the 'Sanhedrin Council.' The *Sanhedrin Council* was the Supreme Court in ancient Israel. It was comprised of seventy men, in addition to the high priest. The *high priest* presided over the Council's proceedings, both civil and criminal. At the time of Jesus the high priest was *Caiaphas*. He, along with his father-in-law *Annas*, spearheaded the hostility against Jesus and criticism of Jesus. The *Sanhedrin Council* included men who were Pharisees, Sadducees, scribes, chief priests, and elders. During the time of Jesus, it had jurisdiction only over the province of Judea. The *Sanhedrin Council* had its own police force that could arrest people, as they would later do in the Garden of Gethsemane with Jesus. While it heard both civil and criminal cases and could impose the death penalty, in New Testament times the *Sanhedrin Council* did not have the authority to execute individuals convicted of a crime. This power was reserved for the Romans, which explains why Jesus was crucified. Crucifixion was a form of Roman punishment and not Jewish law. Stoning was the execution method according to Jewish law. Therefore, the Jews handed Jesus over to the Romans to be crucified.

It is interesting that most times the factions of the *Sanhedrin Council* did not agree with each other, both politically and religiously; however, they all came together for the common purpose of ridding themselves of *Jesus*. To the prevailing religious forces Jesus was a threat. His ministry loosened the control the religious leaders once had on the people. Jesus often criticized the religious leaders for their hypocrisy, and because they often placed burdens on the people they were unwilling to endure themselves. Hear what Jesus says about them: *"They crush people with unbearable religious demands and never lift a finger to ease the burden"* (Matthew 23:4, NLT). Hear what He says in Matthew 23:27, *"Woe to you, teachers of the law and Pharisees, you hypocrites! You are like whitewashed tombs, which look beautiful on the outside but on the inside are full of [dead] bones and everything unclean"* (NIV). This repertoire of condemnation was often leveled against them by Jesus, and oh how they hated Jesus. Because of their hatred of Jesus they sought to derail His ministry. In seeking to do so many times they interrupted His teachings, challenged His miracles, interrogated His followers, and questioned His authority. When these efforts failed, all five groups (Pharisees, Sadducees, scribes, chief priests, elders) and the high priest conspired to kill Jesus. They wanted Him dead, not knowing that Jesus' death would fulfill God's plan to bring salvation to the world. Jesus says, *"And I, if I be lifted up from the earth, will draw all men unto Me"* (John 12:32).

The confrontation between Jesus and the religious leaders occurs at the climax of Jesus' ministry, merely days from His death on a cross. It follows Jesus' triumphant entry into Jerusalem, His cleansing of the temple, and His healing of the blind and the lame in the temple courtyard. We are told, *"He healed them all"* (v. 14). The confrontation also follows Jesus' lesson of the withered fig tree. This tree was cursed by Jesus when it failed to produce for Jesus, like some of us, the fruit it was crafted to give. This withering astonished Jesus' disciples, so Jesus gave them a lesson on faith and prayer. He tells them, as well as us through Scripture, *"Whatever things you ask in prayer, believing, you will receive"* (v. 22). The message: "Only Believe." All things are possible if we believe.

Upon returning to the temple from a night of rest at Bethany, while teaching Jesus is encountered by the chief priests and elders who question His authority and the source of His authority. However, as Jesus often did when challenged, He challenged those who challenged Him. Jesus propositions a "quid pro quo." He would answer their question if they would answer one from Him. Jesus was a master at flip-flopping situations and silencing adversaries with His piercing questions. He says, *"John's baptism— where did it come from, was it from Heaven or of men"* (v.25)? This question places the religious leaders in a dilemma. The dilemma was—whatever answer they gave would incriminate them. We are told, *"They discussed it among themselves"* (v. 25). In other words, they huddled up because they knew they had a problem: *"If we say, 'from Heaven,' He will say to us, 'why then did you not believe him?' If we say, 'from men,' we fear the multitude"* (vv. 25-26). The multitude acknowledged John the Baptist as a prophet. So the religious leaders said, *"We do not know"* (v. 27), and Jesus says to them, *"neither will I tell you by what authority I do these things"* (v. 27). But let me tell you a story and tell me what you think. It is a 'tale of two sons.'

> A certain man had two sons, and he came to the first and said, 'Son, go, work today in my vineyard.' He answered and said, 'I will not,' but afterward he regretted it and went; then he came to the second and said likewise, and he answered and said, 'I go, sir,' but he did not go. Which of the two did the will of his father?
>
> vv. 28-31

The answer is obvious, *"the first"* (v. 31), which is the answer they give. Jesus then shares the point of the parable.

The religious leaders were self-righteous and in need of repentance. They were like the son who said "I go sir," but did nothing. They despised others and rejected the true salvation of God—Jesus. John the Baptist recognized Jesus as God's salvation when he said, *"Behold the Lamb of God, which taketh away the sin of the world"* (John 1:29). Jesus told His challengers, *"tax collectors and prostitutes shall enter the Kingdom of God ahead of you"* (v. 31, NIV), *"for John came to you in the way of righteousness, and you did not believe him; but tax collectors and harlots believed him; and when you saw it, you did not afterward relent and believe him"* (v. 32).

Tax collectors and harlots heard. Tax collectors and harlots believed. Tax collectors and harlots repented, but not you. What is the point of the parable? *"A certain man had two sons"* (Matthew 21:28), and each of us are one of them. Concerning the Will of God, we either do or we do not, we either will or we will not. Some say "yes" and do nothing. Some say "no," but repent and do the will of God. The point is: It is not what we say but what we do that makes the difference. 'Talk is cheap.' Lip service does not please God. God wants us to obey Him. *"Faith without works is dead"* (James 2:26). Who does the will of God? Is it the person who says "I will" and does not, or the one who says "I will not," but does. The answer is clear, but the question remains, "Which son are you?"

The parable is a challenge for the people of God to be about our Father's business. It is a challenge to work. It is a challenge to witness. It is a challenge to obey. It is a challenge to submit. Jesus is challenging us to surrender our will into the hands of God. He challenges sinners to hear, believe, and repent. He challenges believers to move beyond a bogus commitment. *Bogus* means fake. *Bogus* means fraudulent. *Bogus* means phony. *Bogus* means fictitious. Who did the will of the father? What was said? What was done? One intended to do it, but he did not. The lesson: Intentions are not good enough. One declined, but changed his mind and worked. The lesson: It is action, not conversation that gets the work done. Which son are you? The *harvest is still ripe* and workers are still needed. God is calling us into His vineyard of lost souls and into His vineyard of hurting lives. The question is: *will you go?* The question is: *will you obey?* The question is: *will you hear God's Word, receive God's Word,* and *submit to God's work?* WHICH SON ARE YOU?

CHAPTER 14

PAY THE RENT!
Parable of the Wicked Vinedressers

Matthew 21:33-46 NLT

33 "Now listen to another story. A certain landowner planted a vineyard, built a wall around it, dug a pit for pressing out the grape juice, and built a lookout tower. Then he leased the vineyard to tenant farmers and moved to another country. 34 At the time of the grape harvest, he sent his servants to collect his share of the crop. 35 But the farmers grabbed his servants, beat one, killed one, and stoned another. 36 So the landowner sent a larger group of his servants to collect for him, but the results were the same. 37 "Finally, the owner sent his son, thinking, 'Surely they will respect my son.' 38 "But when the tenant farmers saw his son coming, they said to one another, 'Here comes the heir to this estate. Come on, let's kill him and get the estate for ourselves!' 39 So they grabbed him, dragged him out of the vineyard, and murdered him. 40 "When the owner of the vineyard returns," Jesus asked, "what do you

think he will do to those farmers?" [41] The religious leaders replied, "He will put the wicked men to a horrible death and lease the vineyard to others who will give him his share of the crop after each harvest." [42] Then Jesus asked them, "Didn't you ever read this in the Scriptures? 'The stone that the builders rejected has now become the cornerstone. This is the LORD's doing, and it is wonderful to see.' [43] I tell you, the Kingdom of God will be taken away from you and given to a nation that will produce the proper fruit. [44] Anyone who stumbles over that stone will be broken to pieces, and it will crush anyone it falls on." [45] When the leading priests and Pharisees heard this parable, they realized He was telling the story against them— they were the wicked farmers. [46] They wanted to arrest Him, but they were afraid of the crowds, who considered Jesus to be a prophet.

<hr />

The story of this chapter is another parable by Jesus that immediately follows the parable discussed in the last chapter. Jesus is still in the temple at Jerusalem days before His crucifixion. He is teaching His disciples and the multitude that surrounded Him the expectations of God's Kingdom. He also heals the blind and the lame in the courtyard of the temple (see verse 14). It is here, as we noted in last chapter, Jesus is confronted by delegates from the religious community. These religious leaders interrupt His teaching to question His authority. They demanded to know what right Jesus had to dismantle their marketplace, and what right He had to heal and teach in the temple. From their perspective, the temple and its perimeters were areas under their control, and who was this Galilean to drive out the money changers and those who sold and purchased in the marketplace. The religious leaders were angry because Jesus was interfering with their profitable business of making money—of making money through corrupt and sacrilegious practices. So they question Jesus with stern indignation: *"By what authority are You doing these things? And who gave You this authority"* (v. 23)? However, the inquisition was only an attempt to ensnare Jesus. The religious leaders wanted to indict Jesus of some crime that would result in a verdict of death against Jesus. The time was near for Jesus to give His life, and these Jewish rulers were eager to take it. So they approach Jesus with an agenda to arrest Jesus.

When questioned, as we stated in the last chapter, Jesus offers a *quid pro quo*, which in Latin means "something for something." As the religious leaders questioned Jesus' authority, Jesus posed a question concerning the ministry of John the Baptist. His question placed them in a predicament among the people, who viewed John the Baptist as a prophet. To the question of Jesus they gave no answer and, in reply, Jesus gives no answer. Instead, Jesus tells a story about a man who had two sons. In fact, Jesus shares a series of stories to express the fact that He was God's Son operating by God's authority. One of these stories is the story within Matthew 21:33-46. It is called *The Parable of the Wicked Tenants*. Before we continue, it is only appropriate that we consider the responsibility of *tenants*. In essence, all of us are tenants in God's world. *"The earth is the LORD's, and the fulness thereof; the world, and they that dwell therein"* (Psalm 24:1). *"In the beginning God created the heaven and the earth"* (Genesis 1:1), and as Creator, God is the Owner, Titleholder, Proprietor, and Landlord.

From Genesis through Revelation it is clear that the world is God's and we are but leaseholders. Therefore, the parable has a message for us, as well as for those who questioned the authority of Jesus. It has a message for us because some of us are too much like the tenants of the parable. In other words, we act as if the world and the church belong to us. However, the world and the church, and everything attached to both belong to God. All that we possess is provided by God. He owns everything. We own nothing. The parable speaks to us because some of us, like the tenants of the parable, are resentful when reminded by those sent from God of our obligations to God—of our obligations to pay our tithes—of our obligations to help others out—of our obligations to fellowship with the saints—of our obligations to love God with our whole heart, mind, soul, and strength—of our obligations to love our neighbor as we love ourselves. But whether we like it or not, like the tenants in the parable, we are indebted to God. In other words, we owe God rent and we should pay up. If we are behind, we should bring our payments up-to-date.

Let me define a *tenant*. A 'tenant' is a person who occupies land or property rented from a *landlord*. A 'landlord' is the property owner who allows a tenant to rent his or her property for a contracted period and amount. The renter, once he or she agrees on the contracted terms, is then given custody of the land or the property with the obligation to pay rent. What we generally pay in rent is money; however, the rent in the parable was a share of the produce that was grown on the land. In essence, the tenants in the parable were *sharecroppers*. A 'sharecropper' is a tenant farmer who gives a part of each crop as rent, and in honor of *Black History Month*, let me interject the place of *sharecropping* within black history in America.

After the abolition of slavery white landowners attempted to reestablish a labor force, but a conflict arose between them and blacks who were seeking economic independence. Many former slaves expected the federal government to give them a certain amount of land as compensation for all the work they had done during the slavery era. Some were granted 40 acres of land, and the Union Army also donated some of its mules that were unneeded for battle purposes. This is where we get the expression "40 acres and a mule." But during Reconstruction after the Civil War, the conflict over labor resulted in the sharecropping system, in which black families would rent small plots of land in return for a portion of their crop. The payment of crop was given to the landowner generally at the end of each year. This has been a Black History moment. Let us get back to the parable. In the parable, the agreement between the *landowner* and the *tenant farmers* was also a share of the crop harvested from the land. The landowner leased his vineyard to tenant farmers and then moved to another country. Still he expected rent to be paid.

Jesus does not communicate this story for no reason. Each character in the story represents an actual personality or people. In the parable there is a landowner. The *landowner* embodies God. In the parable there is a vineyard. The *vineyard* symbolizes the nation of Israel. In the parable there are tenants. The *tenants* depict the religious leaders. In the parable there are servants. The *servants* are the many prophets sent by God, inclusive of John the Baptist. The son, of course, is Jesus. When the parable states that the landowner planted a vineyard, built a wall around it, dug a pit for pressing out the grape juice and built a lookout tower, it gives reference to the provision and protection of God. God placed Israel in a land that was 'flowing with milk and honey' (see Exodus 33:3). It was a land that had been prepared by God for Israel to yield in abundance. The only thing God required of Israel was 'righteous fruit.' In other words, in exchange for His divine goodness and generosity, God wanted a people who would obey Him. He wanted a people who would please Him. He wanted a people who would exemplify Him. He wanted a people who would honor Him. He wanted a people who would live right before Him. This is the 'fruit' that God expected of His people then, which is the same 'fruit' God expects of His people now. We are those people.

Today God desires from us what He desired from Israel— obedience and a righteous lifestyle. We too, like the Israelites, are called to be a chosen generation, a royal priesthood, a holy nation, and a peculiar people (see Exodus 19:5-6; 1 Peter 2:9). We too have the responsibility of divine ambassadorship. We too are expected to conduct ourselves in accordance with God's instructions for our lives. We too are to reverence those sent by God who teach us the ways of God. We too are to surrender to God whatever God asks for. We too are expected to *pay rent*. We cannot reap the benefits of Godly resources without rendering what we owe Him. God blesses us with *time*, but He wants some of it back. God blesses us with *treasures*, but He wants some of it back. God blesses us with *talents*, but He wants some of it back. He wants us to *pay rent!*

The meaning of the parable was no secret. It was directed at those who were entrusted with God's people and God's commandments. The chief priests were in charge of temple worship and obligated with the responsibility of setting the standard of godly behavior. But they were crooked, corrupt, deceitful, and sanctimonious. They rejected the message of John the Baptist and scorned the ministry of Jesus. They killed John and were now plotting to murder Jesus. They were like the wicked tenants in the parable who beat, stoned, and killed the servants, and then the son. But Jesus was aware of their intentions, and the parable is told to expose them. The parable is also told to prophecy the fate that awaited them who would take liberty to kill Jesus. Some forty years later Jerusalem would fall. Some forty years later the temple would be destroyed. In forty years the Landowner (God) would return to take vengeance for His Son

(Jesus).The message is: "Pay the rent!" Don't anger God. Don't snub the Son. Give God what is due Him.

What we have is not ours. What we hold belongs to God. We owe God for His goodness. We owe God for His grace. We owe God for His mercy. We owe God twice. We owe God for life and new life. We owe God for salvation. We owe God for redemption. We owe God for forgiveness. We owe God for Calvary. The message is: "Pay the rent!" Jesus was wounded for our transgressions. We owe God. Jesus was bruised for our iniquities. We owe God. He was crucified on a cross and He died for our sins. We owe God. The message is: "Pay the rent!" The rent is obedience. The rent is gratitude. The rent is worship. The rent is everything we owe God that God decrees we should give Him. Pay the rent! Make a joyful noise unto the LORD. Pay the rent! Sing unto Him a new song. Pay the rent! Let your light so shine before men. Pay the rent! Be a witness throughout the world. Pay the rent! All to Jesus I surrender. All to Him I freely give. The rent is commitment. The rent is love. The rent is sacrifice. The rent is faithfulness. God deserves our very best. Pay the rent! God deserves our whole heart. Pay the rent! Do not get caught with your work undone. Do not stand before the Lord empty-handed. Do not give God your leftovers. Give God the firstfruits. Pay the rent!

Pay the rent with your tithes. Pay the rent with your service. Pay the rent with your praise. Pay the rent with a holy lifestyle. The Apostle Paul says,

I beseech you therefore, brethren, by the mercies of God, that ye present your bodies a living sacrifice, holy, acceptable unto God, which is your reasonable service. And be not conformed to this world: but be ye transformed by the renewing of your mind, that ye may prove what is that good, and acceptable, and perfect, will of God.

Romans 12:1-2

It is time to pay the rent! It is time to live for God. It is time to represent God. It is time to submit to God. If you want to hear the Lord say, "Servant well done," the rent must be paid. Do not hold back. Do not short-change God. Do not renege on your vow. Pay up! Pay the rent! Bring the rent up-to-date! Jesus went away, but Jesus is coming back to collect. He is coming back for His church without spot or wrinkle. The Landlord is on His way. PAY THE RENT!

CHAPTER 15

DON'T TAKE GOD'S GRACE FOR GRANTED
Parable of the Wedding Feast

Matthew 22:1-14

¹And Jesus answered and spoke to them again by parables and said: ² "The Kingdom of Heaven is like a certain king who arranged a marriage for his son, ³ and sent out his servants to call those who were invited to the wedding; and they were not willing to come. ⁴ Again, he sent out other servants, saying, 'Tell those who are invited, "See, I have prepared my dinner; my oxen and fatted cattle are killed, and all things are ready. Come to the wedding."' ⁵ But they made light of it and went their ways, one to his own farm, another to his business. ⁶ And the rest seized his servants, treated them spitefully, and killed them. ⁷ But when the king heard about it, he was furious. And he sent out his armies, destroyed those murderers, and burned up their city. ⁸ Then he said to his servants, 'The wedding is ready, but those who were invited were not worthy. ⁹ Therefore go into the highways, and as many as you find, invite to the

wedding.' [10] So those servants went out into the highways and gathered together all whom they found, both bad and good. And the wedding hall was filled with guests. [11] "But when the king came in to see the guests, he saw a man there who did not have on a wedding garment. [12] So he said to him, 'Friend, how did you come in here without a wedding garment?' And he was speechless. [13] Then the king said to the servants, 'Bind him hand and foot, take him away, and cast him into outer darkness; there will be weeping and gnashing of teeth.' [14] "For many are called, but few are chosen."

<hr/>

The setting of this chapter's story is once again within the temple at Jerusalem just days before the event of Calvary. Even as Jesus approaches death, He takes the time to illustrate through story the expectations of the Kingdom. The reason Jesus does so is because He wanted His disciples to know for certain what was required of them, as well as of those who would believe on Him through their words. To the disciples it was given to know the mysteries of God's Kingdom, and parables safeguarded these mysteries from insincere individuals with ulterior motives (see Matthew 13:10-11; Mark 4:10-11; Luke 8:9-10).

The story of Matthew 22:1-14 is known as *The Parable of the Wedding Feast*, and it is the third of three parables Jesus told when challenged by the religious leaders during His final week before the cross. In the last two chapters I expounded on the other two parables, the *Parable of the Two Sons* and the *Parable of the Wicked*

Tenants. The *Two Sons* parable was told because of the religious leaders' rejection of John the Baptist (see Matthew 21:23-32), and the *Wicked Tenants* story describes how God would reject them and all others who rejected His prophets, inclusive of John, and ultimately His own Son (see Matthew 21:33-46). In the *Wedding Feast* narrative, Jesus unveils Himself and the religious leaders' rejection of Him even more, as well as the punishment that would ensue through the fury of an angry God.

In the previous parable, the *Parable of the Wicked Tenants*, Jesus is the son of a landowner who is cast out of the vineyard and killed. In this parable, the *Parable of the Wedding Feast*, He is also the son, but depicted as the Son of a King. In the previous parable what was owed went unpaid. In this parable what is offered is spurned. *Spurn* means to "reject with disdain or contempt." It means "to despise." It means "to scorn." It means "to refuse." It means "to treat as insignificant." In the previous parable, judgment is rendered for rejection and murder. In this parable it is also dispensed for rejection and murder, but expanded to include those who make light of the invitation of the King and the wedding feast of His Son. The message is: Do not refuse the offer. The message is: Do not trivialize its importance. The message is: Do not attack the messengers. The message is: Do not take God's grace for granted. In transitioning from one parable to another Jesus says, *"The Kingdom of Heaven is like a certain king who arranged a marriage for his son"* (v. 2). This marriage arrangement is emblematic of the 'Marriage Supper of the Lamb.' The *Marriage Supper of the Lamb* is foretold in the Book of Revelation

Chapter 19. There it is written, *"Blessed are those who are called to the marriage supper of the Lamb"* (v. 9). In other words, *"Blessed are those who are invited"* (NLT).

An invitation to a royal wedding is often a once-in-a-lifetime experience, and people who get such an invitation are overwhelmed with excitement and joy. Such an invitation is rarely, if ever, turned down. In fact, people will spend big money for an invitation to a royal wedding. In recent years it was reported that a young English girl went on a hunger strike trying to get her hands on an invitation. A royal wedding is a big affair, and what kind of person would shun an invitation to a royal wedding? But as we look at the wedding invitees within our text, we see refusal. We see mockery. We see homicide and even inappropriate attire for the occasion. We could teach a lesson on *inappropriate attire*, especially when you examine the way some people dress going to church. This is not to say that you have to wear a suit and tie or a dress down to your ankles, but the *church house* is not the lounge. The *church house* is not the dance hall. The *church house* is not the strip club. The *church house* is not the whore house. In other words, we should not go to church dressed like pimps and prostitutes, or exotic dancers, body builders, and hoochie mamas. You know what a 'hoochie mama' is? A *hoochie mama* is the ghetto version of a *gold digger* and dresses 'ghetto ho fabulous.' They wear lots of gold, and lots of weave, and lots of colors, and long nails with lots of airbrush glitter—revealing everything and hiding nothing—out trolling for sugar daddies at parties, and trolling the streets for someone to pay the rent—GHETTO HO FABULOUS. Do not get mad at me. This is the definition in the urban dictionary for *hoochie mama*. I just looked it up and inserted the characterization into this lesson.

I may be old-fashioned, but I think when we go to church we should dress in apparel suitable for coming into the presence of a holy God. I think we should cover up some stuff. I think we should close up some stuff. I think we should loosen up some stuff. I think we should recognize where we are. The church house is the Lord's House and we should reverence the Lord's House as the Lord's House! God's demand is: *"Be holy, because I am holy"* (Leviticus 11:44, NIV). I know holiness is a lifestyle, but a holy lifestyle would not put its flesh on display. Enough said. Let us get back to the text. Who would turn down a royal invitation?

Can you imagine if *William* and *Kate* had sent out thousands of invitations, only to arrive at Westminster Abbey to an empty church? It would never happen. People were fighting for an invitation to that wedding, as they did for William's parents, *Charles* and *Diana*. But in Jesus' story the people not only blew off the wedding, they also beat and killed the individuals who hand-delivered the invitations. These 'invitation carriers' represent the prophets of old and preachers of now, who bring to the people the Word of God—the Word of repentance—the Word of salvation—the Word of redemption—the Good news of Jesus Christ. Those who say, "The door of the Church is open." Those who say, "Come, all who are weary." Those who say, "Now is the acceptable time." Those who signal sinners to the Cross. Those who declare, *"For God so loved the world, that He gave His only begotten Son, that whosoever believeth in Him should not perish, but have everlasting life"* (John 3:16). This is the message we deliver. This is the memo dictated from Heaven. It is an invitation to the Wedding of all weddings—to the *Marriage Supper of the Lamb*. God is the King and Jesus is the Groom. The Bride is the Church, and the Church is made up of anyone who will come—of anyone who will receive the invitation of the Cross. The invitation reads: *"Come to Me, all you who labor and are heavy laden, and I will give you rest"* (Matthew 11:28). The invitation reads: "Whosoever will, let him or her come." But come with the right attire. Do not come underdressed. This is a royal wedding. You cannot choose your own wardrobe. The Wedding invitation has a dress code, and the dress code is 'holiness.' The dress code is 'righteousness.' The dress code is 'sanctification.' The dress code is 'a consecrated life.' The Apostle Paul declares,

> I beseech you therefore, brethren, by the mercies of God, that ye present your bodies a living sacrifice, holy, acceptable unto God, which is your reasonable service. And be not conformed to this world: but be ye transformed by the renewing of your mind, that ye may prove what is that good, and acceptable, and perfect, will of God.
>
> Romans 12:1-2

At the Wedding, Jesus wants to present to the Father a glorious

Church, without spot or wrinkle (see Ephesians 5:27). At the Wedding, Jesus wants to hand over to the Father a people who have not compromised their faith, or denied their Savior, or abandoned their testimony, or tarnished their character and reputation. And the question is: "Are you dressed right?" The question is: "Are you ready?" The question is: "Will you accept?" The question is: "Will you show up?" In God's Word is an invitation and it is addressed to 'whosoever.' To whosoever will believe. To whosoever will receive. To whosoever will come. To whosoever will live right. It is for the fisherman and the tax-collector. It is for the outcast and ostracized. It is for the rich and the poor. It is for the homeless and incarcerated. It is for the sick. It is for the lame. It is for the deaf, blind, and the dumb. It is for blacks. It is for whites. It is for men and women. It is an invitation to a Royal Wedding, and *"many are called, but few are chosen"* (Matthew 22:14). So do not take it for granted. Do not reject it or laugh at it. Do not ignore it or misuse it. It is God's grace, so appreciate it. It is God's grace, embrace it. It is God's grace, be grateful. It is God's grace, consent to it. It cost too much. It required too much. It demanded too much. God gave up too much. What did He give up? God gave up His Son! His Royal Son!

The Cross is God's grace. Calvary is His sacrifice. There Jesus died for our sins. There Jesus suffered in our place. There *"He was wounded for our transgressions"* (Isaiah 53:5). There *"He was bruised for our iniquities"* (Isaiah 53:5). We are saved by grace. We are healed by grace. We are redeemed by grace, and by the grace of God we are still here. God's grace is His love. God's grace is His forgiveness. God's grace is His mercy. It is His Hands in our lives. Grace wakes us up in the mornings. Grace gives us another chance. Grace cleanses us, and renews us, and grace changes us for the better. Grace is free. Grace is available. Grace is unconditional. Grace indeed is God's gift. So do not take grace for granted. Do not make light of God's kindness. It is amazing! It is abundant! It is universal! It is God's favor!

Grace is the reason we are here. Grace is the reason we are saved. Grace is the reason we have been reconciled. Grace is the reason our names are written in the *Lamb's Book of Life*. So DO NOT TAKE GRACE FOR GRANTED! Welcome it. Acknowledge it. Accept it. Praise God for His Amazing Grace! *"Amazing grace, how sweet the sound, that saved a wretch like me! I once was lost, but now am found; was blind, but now I see"* (Hymn, John Newton). DO NOT TAKE GOD'S GRACE FOR GRANTED! Do not play with it. Do not laugh at it. Do not neglect it or despise it. But celebrate grace. Be glad for grace. Rejoice over grace, and be thankful to God. DO NOT TAKE GOD'S GRACE FOR GRANTED!

EPILOGUE

"And they lived happily ever after." This is the conclusion most love to hear; however, not every story has a happy ending. The stories Jesus told only benefit those willing to receive the message they communicate. His stories are filled with memorable characters and common human conditions and situations, all designed to bring divine revelation, inspiration, information, instruction, and or conviction with the intent of conversion. But the transmission or transformation depend upon the receptibility of the hearer. In Matthew 11:15 Jesus says, *"Anyone with ears to hear should listen and understand"* (NLT).

Those who opposed Jesus approached Him with hardened hearts. A *hardened heart* is a spiritual condition that inhibits a person from hearing, seeing, understanding, and detecting that which is spiritual. A hardened heart dulls an individual's ability to perceive and understand spiritual matters—people in such state only rationalize that which is natural or carnal. This malady is substantiated by Scripture. First Corinthians 2:14 state,

> But the natural man does not accept the things of the Spirit of God, for they are folly to him, and he is not able to understand them because they are spiritually discerned.

Romans 8:7 declare, "The carnal mind is enmity against God; for it is not subject to the law of God, nor indeed can be."

A 'carnal mind' is a mind that is dictated and directed by what our five senses (*see, hear, touch, smell, and feel*) express to us. It is a mind of the flesh—a worldly mind—a mind that contradicts the Word of God. In contrast, a spiritual mind submits to the will of God as directed by the Spirit of God through the Word of God. Its diet and delight is in the law of the LORD, and in His law it meditates day and night (see Psalm 1:2).

It is my pray that what I have spoken through the stories Jesus told will be embraced with an opened heart and hungry spirit. I do not share these lessons to entertain, but to edify. I share these lessons to further broadcast the lessons Jesus taught in hopes of awakening a generation, and future generations to what God continues to expect of us who pledge allegiance to Him. Remember, we are "the salt of the earth" (Matthew 5:13) and "the light of the world" (Matthew 5:14). The *Kingdom of God* is felt and seen by and through us. We are to be the sheep, Good Samaritans, friends at midnight, wise virgins, faithful stewards, forgiving fathers, seed sowers, persistent widows, and all other good personalities of Jesus' parables that reflect the will of God.

Do not allow sin, especially the sin of pride, to grow your heart hard. Let the stories of Jesus speak to you and transform your life, lifestyle, mind, and behavior. In this book I have only shared a few stories. There are many more that Jesus told. Read and study the Gospel accounts of Matthew, Mark, Luke, and John. Take a sit on the hillside, or by the seashore, or in the garden and temple courtyard. Hear what the Spirit has to say through the stories Jesus told. If you listen with a thirst, a story will fill your soul.

More Books by Larry A. Brookins

It's All About the Kingdom, Volume One

Seven Things God Hates & Seven Letters to Seven Churches

The Detox Series: Decontaminating the Soul

Becoming a Five-Star Church: Transforming into a Ministry of Excellence

Becoming a Five-Star Member: Answering the Call of All Hands on Deck

Discipleship: From Bond Leather to Shoe Leather

The Tabernacle: Where Humanity Meets Divinity

Evangelism: The Church in Sync with God

The Fruit of the Spirit: A Cluster of Christ-like Characters

Gifts of the Spirit: Divine Endowments for the Body of Christ

The Biblical Deacon Training Manual

The Deaconess Training Manual

Seven Things that God Hates Companion Workbook

Seven Letters to Seven Churches Companion Workbook

Tithing: A Workbook on Biblical Giving

Lord Teach Us to Pray: Gleaning from the Instructions of Jesus

Understanding the Ordinances of Baptism & the Lord's Supper

VISIT
www.labrookinsministries.org

LIFE TO LEGACY LLC

Let us bring your story to life! Life to Legacy offers the following publishing services: manuscript development, editing, transcription services, ghostwriting, cover design, copyright services, ISBN assignment, worldwide distribution, and eBooks.

Throughout the entire production process, you maintain control over your project. Even if you have no manuscript, we can ghostwrite your story for you from audio recordings or legible handwritten documents. Whether print-on-demand or trade publishing, we have publishing packages to meet your needs. We make the production and publishing processes easy for you.

We also specialize in family history books, so you can leave a written legacy for your children, grandchildren, and others. You put your story in our hands, and we'll bring it to literary life!

Please visit our website:
www.Life2Legacy.com

Or call us at:
877-267-7477

You can also send email to:
Life2Legacybooks@att.net

CPSIA information can be obtained at www.ICGtesting.com
Printed in the USA
LVOW08s0402260515

439551LV00002B/2/P